AF454261

THE NIGERIAN DATA BLUEPRINT

Shefiu Yusuf

TABLE OF CONTENTS

PREFACE

Data has become the oil of the 21st century, a critical resource driving innovation, growth, and transformation across industries and nations. It powers economies, shapes policies, and creates opportunities that were unimaginable just a few decades ago. Yet, like oil, data must be refined, processed, and harnessed strategically to unlock its true potential. For Nigeria, a country endowed with immense human and natural resources, the journey toward a data-driven future is both urgent and promising.

The global landscape is evolving rapidly. Every sector, from healthcare and agriculture to governance and entertainment, is being transformed by the power of data. However, Nigeria risks being left behind if we do not act decisively to build the infrastructure, skills, and policies necessary to integrate data into our national framework. The stakes are high. A data-driven Nigeria is not a luxury; it is a necessity for our survival in a competitive global economy.

This book, "The Nigerian Data Blueprint," is the culmination of years of experience, observation, and research. It is born out of a firm belief that the future of our nation depends on how effectively we use data to make informed decisions, drive economic growth, and improve the quality of life for all citizens. Nigeria's potential is enormous but realizing it will require a concerted effort from all stakeholders', policymakers, educators, entrepreneurs, and citizens alike.

My journey into the world of data began with a fascination for its transformative power. Over the years, I have witnessed firsthand how data can solve complex problems, streamline processes, and create new opportunities. Yet, I have also seen how the lack of data or the inability to use it effectively can exacerbate challenges and widen inequalities.

This book is not merely a technical manual; it is a vision for Nigeria's future; a future where data empowers businesses, enhances governance, and uplifts communities. It is my hope that this blueprint will inspire readers to think differently about data and to see it not as an abstract concept but as a tangible tool for change.

In writing this book, I have drawn insights from a diverse range of fields, including technology, education, public policy, and entrepreneurship. Each chapter explores a different facet of the data ecosystem, offering practical strategies and actionable steps for building a data-driven Nigeria. From overcoming infrastructure challenges to fostering a culture of data literacy, the blueprint is comprehensive and grounded in the realities of our nation.

To those who pick up this book, I extend an invitation: join the conversation. Share your insights, challenge the ideas presented here, and contribute to the collective effort of building a brighter future for Nigeria. Together, we can ensure that data becomes a force for good—a tool for development, innovation, and inclusion.

FOREWORD

In a world increasingly defined by technology and information, the importance of data cannot be overstated. Data is the new currency, the foundation upon which modern economies are built. Nations that fail to harness the power of data risk being left behind, unable to compete in a rapidly changing global landscape.

Nigeria, with its dynamic population and burgeoning economy, stands at a crossroads. On the one hand, we have a wealth of untapped potential: a young and vibrant workforce, a growing tech ecosystem, and abundant natural resources. On the other hand, we face significant challenges: inadequate infrastructure, low data literacy, and a lack of cohesive policies to support data-driven development.

"The Nigerian Data Blueprint" by Shefiu Yusuf is a timely and indispensable guide to understanding how Nigeria can unlock the potential of data for national growth and development. It is a book that speaks not only to policymakers and technocrats but to anyone who cares about the future of our nation. Through clear insights, actionable strategies, and a deep understanding of Nigeria's unique challenges, this book provides a roadmap for navigating the complexities of the digital age.

What sets this book apart is its holistic approach. Shefiu Yusuf does not simply advocate for more technology or better infrastructure. Instead, he recognizes that building a data-driven nation requires a multifaceted strategy that addresses education, governance, ethics, and culture. His vision is both ambitious and achievable, a testament to his deep commitment to Nigeria's progress.

I commend Shefiu for his dedication to this cause and for providing us with a work that is both thought-provoking and practical. The lessons in this book are not confined to Nigeria; they resonate with any nation seeking to harness the power of data for development. However, the focus on Nigeria makes it particularly valuable for our context, offering solutions that are tailored to our needs and aspirations.

As you read "The Nigerian Data Blueprint," I encourage you to think about your role in this journey. Whether you are a policymaker, an entrepreneur, an educator, or a student, you have a part to play in building a data-driven Nigeria. The future is data-driven, and Nigeria must lead the way.

INTRODUCTION

Nigeria is a nation of immense potential. With over two hundred million people, a thriving youth population, and a diverse economy, we are uniquely positioned to become a global leader. Yet, despite our abundant resources, we face persistent challenges: economic instability, inadequate infrastructure, and inefficiencies in governance. The solution to many of these challenges lies in one powerful tool: data.

Data is more than numbers and statistics; it is the foundation of informed decision-making. Whether it is mapping healthcare needs, predicting agricultural trends, or driving business innovation, data offers the insights we need to thrive. Yet, Nigeria's data ecosystem remains underdeveloped, plagued by issues such as lack of access, poor infrastructure, and limited literacy.

This book aims to address these gaps. "The Nigerian Data Blueprint" explores how we can build a robust data ecosystem that empowers citizens, drives innovation, and fosters sustainable growth. From government policy to grassroots education, each chapter outlines specific strategies for transforming Nigeria into a data-driven nation.

Globally, data is reshaping industries and economies. From predictive analytics in healthcare to AI-driven financial services, data is the engine driving innovation. In Nigeria, however, many sectors are still operating without reliable data, leading to inefficiencies and missed opportunities. For example, our agricultural sector, which employs a significant portion of the population, lacks the data infrastructure needed to optimize production and distribution.

Imagine a Nigeria where data drives decision-making in every sector. Hospitals equipped with real-time data systems deliver better patient care. Farmers use predictive analytics to increase crop yields. Policymakers make informed decisions based on accurate data, leading to more effective governance.

This is the vision of "The Nigerian Data Blueprint." It is a vision rooted in optimism and grounded in practicality. As you turn the pages, you will discover a roadmap for achieving this vision, a roadmap that combines innovation, collaboration, and determination.

CHAPTER 1
THE RISE OF DATA IN A DIGITAL AGE

The 21st century has been characterized by a phenomenon of unprecedented magnitude: the exponential growth of data. Across the globe, the very fabric of modern existence generates data with every action taken every purchase made, every message sent, every search conducted, and every decision reached leaves behind a distinct digital footprint. This expanding ocean of information is not merely an incidental byproduct of human activity but has emerged as a vital resource. In the modern world, data drives innovation, fuels industries, and serves as a cornerstone of economic development on a global scale. Unlike the industrial revolutions of previous centuries, which were defined by the exploitation of physical resources such as coal, oil, and gas, the Fourth Industrial Revolution has ushered in an era where data takes center stage. No longer just a tool, data is a resource that countries must cultivate, refine, and wield strategically to thrive in the digital age.

Around the world, nations are harnessing the power of data to tackle significant societal challenges and secure their positions in a highly competitive global economy. In the United States, a robust and dynamic data ecosystem is dominated by private enterprises that innovate at an astounding pace. These companies have revolutionized industries ranging from healthcare and transportation to finance and entertainment. In China, the approach to data utilization is markedly different but equally transformative. The Chinese government treats data as a central pillar of its strategy for technological advancement, social governance, and urban development. With heavy investment in artificial intelligence, smart cities, and advanced analytics, China has positioned itself as a leading force in the global data economy. Similarly, India has embraced data as a vehicle for progress, fostering inclusive development through groundbreaking initiatives such as Aadhaar, the world's largest biometric identification system. Aadhaar has streamlined access to social services for over a billion people, exemplifying how data can directly improve lives on a massive scale.

Even in resource-constrained environments, data has proven its ability to drive meaningful change. In Africa, for example, innovative solutions are paving the way for progress. Kenya's M-Pesa revolutionized financial inclusion by providing mobile banking services to millions who previously lacked access to traditional banking systems. In South Africa, data analytics has been integrated into healthcare initiatives, enabling predictive measures to combat widespread diseases such as HIV/AIDS. These instances demonstrate the power of data to transform societies, even in regions facing significant challenges. However, while countries like Kenya and South Africa are making strides in leveraging data, others lag behind. Nigeria, Africa's largest economy and most populous nation, is notably slow to embrace the data revolution. This delay comes with significant risks and lost opportunities. The transformative power of data offers solutions to many of Nigeria's pressing issues, but the lack of a coordinated and focused approach has left the nation trailing its peers in this critical area.

The barriers Nigeria faces in becoming a data-driven nation are numerous and complex. Among the most significant challenges are infrastructural deficits. Unreliable electricity supplies, poor internet penetration, and a lack of modern technological infrastructure create bottlenecks that inhibit progress. For example, Nigeria's response to the COVID-19 pandemic was hampered by the absence of real-time health data, leading to delays in resource deployment and exacerbating the crisis. In the agricultural sector, where a significant portion of the population earns its livelihood, the reliance on traditional methods and guesswork—rather than data-driven approaches limits productivity and hampers efficiency. The inability to access reliable data further compounds these issues, leaving many sectors of the economy underperforming relative to their potential.

Beyond infrastructure, deeper cultural and educational challenges further complicate the picture. Data literacy levels remain alarmingly low across Nigeria. This gap extends from policymakers and business leaders to the general public, undermining the country's ability to adopt innovative, data-driven solutions. A lack of understanding about the transformative potential of data contributes to a broader cultural resistance to change. Many decision-makers in both public and private sectors continue to rely on intuition, tradition, and outdated practices, rather than evidence-based strategies informed by data.

Despite these obstacles, Nigeria holds immense potential to succeed in the digital age. The country's youthful and vibrant population is one of its greatest assets. With over 60% of Nigerians under the age of 25, the workforce is primed to lead innovation if equipped with the right skills and opportunities. Additionally, Nigeria's growing tech ecosystem offers a foundation for transformative progress. Tech hubs in cities like Lagos, Abuja, and Kaduna are incubating startups that leverage data to address local challenges. These ventures, although still in their early stages, signal that Nigeria possesses the creativity, talent, and ambition needed to thrive in a data-centric world.

To unlock this potential and fully participate in the global data revolution, Nigeria must embark on a deliberate, multi-pronged strategy to build its data ecosystem. At the core of this effort lies the need for significant investment in infrastructure. Stable electricity and reliable internet connectivity are essential building blocks for a data-driven society. Without these foundational elements, the country's ability to harness the power of data will remain limited. Alongside infrastructure development, education must be prioritized. Nigeria's educational system must evolve to integrate data science, analytics, and related fields into its curricula at every level, from primary schools to universities. Building a generation of data-literate citizens is critical to fostering innovation and enabling long-term economic growth.

Equally important is the creation of clear and enforceable policies to govern the use of data. Ethical considerations such as data privacy, security, and intellectual property must be addressed to ensure public trust and foster innovation. Transparent regulations will also encourage international investment and collaboration, positioning Nigeria as a desirable partner in the global data economy. Public-private partnerships will be instrumental in achieving these goals. The Nigerian government cannot build a robust data-driven economy on its own; collaboration with technology companies, international organizations, and local entrepreneurs is essential to overcome resource and knowledge gaps. Such partnerships can provide the expertise, funding, and momentum required to address critical challenges and unlock new opportunities.

Finally, community engagement and public awareness are crucial for success. Nigerians must understand the value of data and trust that it will be used to enhance their lives. Transparency in how data is collected, stored, and used will foster confidence and encourage participation in data-driven initiatives. By involving citizens in the data revolution, Nigeria can ensure that progress is not only achieved but sustained.

The rise of data in the digital age represents both an opportunity and a challenge for nations around the world. For Nigeria, the stakes are particularly high. Embracing data as a strategic resource offers a path to addressing some of the country's most persistent problems, from economic stagnation to inefficient governance. However, the window of opportunity is narrowing. To avoid being left behind, Nigeria must act decisively and strategically to position itself as a leader in the global data economy. This chapter has outlined the foundational importance of data in the modern era and its potential to reshape Nigeria's future. In the chapters ahead, we will delve deeper into the current state of Nigeria's data landscape, exploring its strengths, weaknesses, and the opportunities that lie ahead on this transformative journey.

1.1 The Importance of Investing in Human Capital for a Data-Driven Nigeria

A significant aspect of Nigeria's journey toward becoming a data-driven society lies in the empowerment of its human capital. With one of the youngest populations globally, Nigeria is uniquely positioned to leverage its demographic dividend. This youthful energy represents a reservoir of untapped talent and creativity that could serve as the foundation for a thriving data-driven economy. However, unlocking this potential requires deliberate and targeted interventions that address skill gaps and foster a culture of innovation across various sectors of the economy. From education reform to entrepreneurial support, Nigeria's success in the digital age depends on its ability to empower individuals and communities to harness the power of data.

The development of human capital must begin with overhauling Nigeria's educational system to prioritize digital and data literacy. Traditional curricula focused solely on rote learning are ill-suited for the demands of the Fourth Industrial Revolution. Introducing data science, artificial intelligence, and technology-related subjects at all levels from primary to tertiary education is imperative to building a workforce capable of thriving in an increasingly data-centric world. These subjects must not only teach technical skills but also foster critical thinking, problem-solving, and collaboration, which are essential for innovation.

Additionally, upskilling programs for current professionals are essential to ensure that the existing workforce remains relevant in a rapidly changing economy. As data becomes central to decision-making across industries, employees must transition from traditional roles to more data-oriented positions. These upskilling initiatives could include short courses, workshops, and certifications in areas like data analytics, machine learning, and cloud computing. Partnerships with international educational institutions, online learning platforms, and private sector organizations can make such programs accessible, affordable, and tailored to the needs of Nigerians. These initiatives will not only enhance individual career prospects but also drive economic growth by increasing productivity and innovation.

Entrepreneurship must also play a central role in Nigeria's human capital strategy. Fostering entrepreneurship among young Nigerians can unleash a wave of innovation that addresses local challenges and creates sustainable economic opportunities. By equipping aspiring entrepreneurs with tools, funding, and mentorship, Nigeria can build an ecosystem where data-driven solutions thrive. Hackathons, startup incubators, and accelerator programs can provide young innovators with the resources and networks needed to transform their ideas into impactful businesses. These businesses, in turn, can generate employment, stimulate local industries, and contribute to the overall economic resilience of the nation.

Moreover, empowering women and marginalized groups must be a priority. In many parts of Nigeria, gender disparities and systemic inequities limit access to education and professional opportunities. By ensuring that women and underrepresented communities have equal access to education, training, and entrepreneurial resources, Nigeria can unlock a significant portion of its human capital that has traditionally been overlooked. Inclusive strategies will not only promote social equity but also maximize the country's overall capacity for innovation and growth.

Finally, fostering a culture of lifelong learning is essential to maintaining Nigeria's competitive edge in the global data economy. The rapid pace of technological advancement means that skills acquired today may become obsolete tomorrow. Encouraging continuous professional development through employer-sponsored programs, online learning platforms, and community-based workshops can ensure that Nigerians remain adaptable and equipped to navigate future challenges.

1.2 The Role of International Collaboration in Advancing Nigeria's Data Ecosystem

While domestic initiatives are vital, Nigeria's integration into the global data economy necessitates collaboration with international stakeholders. The challenges of building a robust data ecosystem are complex and multifaceted, requiring expertise, technology, and financial resources that Nigeria cannot fully develop in isolation. By forming strategic partnerships with global leaders in data innovation, Nigeria can accelerate its progress and position itself as a key player in the digital age.

International collaborations can take many forms, each with its unique benefits. Bilateral agreements with leading data-driven nations can facilitate knowledge sharing and the transfer of technology. For example, partnerships with countries like Singapore, Estonia, or Finland renowned for their advanced digital infrastructures can provide valuable insights into building efficient, scalable systems. These partnerships can also pave the way for Nigerian policymakers to learn best practices in data governance, cybersecurity, and ethical AI development, ensuring that Nigeria's data ecosystem is both innovative and secure.

Participation in global forums focused on data governance and innovation is equally important. These platforms allow Nigeria to engage in international discourse, advocate for its interests, and contribute to the development of global standards for data use and regulation. Active participation in such forums not only enhances Nigeria's visibility on the world stage but also positions it as a proactive player in shaping the future of the global data economy.

Foreign direct investment (FDI) into Nigeria's tech and data sectors is another critical component of international collaboration. To attract FDI, the Nigerian government must create a business-friendly environment characterized by clear regulations, tax incentives, and streamlined processes for international companies. Strategic incentives, such as establishing free trade zones focused on technology and data, can further encourage investment. FDI can bring innovative technology, generate employment opportunities, and stimulate the growth of local tech hubs in cities like Lagos, Abuja, and Kaduna.

In addition to attracting investment, Nigeria must actively engage with international development organizations and non-governmental organizations (NGOs) that focus on digital inclusion and capacity building. Collaboration with these organizations can help bridge gaps in funding, infrastructure, and expertise, particularly in underserved and rural areas. By working together on initiatives such as digital literacy campaigns, affordable internet access programs, and data-driven solutions for healthcare and agriculture, Nigeria can ensure that the benefits of the data revolution are equitably distributed across its population.

Global collaboration can also extend to academic and research partnerships. Nigerian universities and research institutions must build connections with their international counterparts to foster innovation and knowledge exchange. Joint research initiatives, faculty exchange programs, and scholarships for Nigerian students to study abroad in data-related fields can help build a cadre of highly skilled professionals who can drive innovation upon their return.

Finally, international partnerships must prioritize sustainability and ethical considerations. The exploitation of developing nations in the global digital economy is a legitimate concern, and Nigeria must ensure that its collaborations are mutually beneficial. Clear agreements on data sovereignty, intellectual property, and resource sharing are essential to safeguarding Nigeria's interests and promoting trust among stakeholders.

By embracing these collaborative strategies, Nigeria can bridge critical gaps in its data ecosystem and accelerate its transition to a data-driven economy. The combination of domestic efforts and international partnerships will enable Nigeria to harness the full potential of data, driving sustainable development and securing its place as a leader in the global digital revolution.

CHAPTER 2
NIGERIA'S CURRENT DATA LANDSCAPE

Nigeria, as Africa's most populous country and largest economy, occupies a unique position with immense potential to harness the power of data for national development. Yet, despite these advantages, the nation's current data landscape is characterized by fragmentation, underutilization, and significant gaps in infrastructure and governance. To chart a path forward, it is essential to understand the present state of data in Nigeria, including its strengths, weaknesses, and untapped opportunities.

The state of Nigeria's data infrastructure reflects the country's broader infrastructural challenges. Internet penetration, though growing, remains uneven, with rural areas particularly underserved. As of recent estimates, only a fraction of the population enjoys reliable broadband access, limiting the ability of businesses, governments, and individuals to collect, process, and utilize data. Moreover, power outages and unreliable electricity compound the problem, making it difficult to sustain data centers and other critical components of a digital ecosystem. Without these foundational elements, the broader ambitions of a data-driven economy are constrained.

Beyond physical infrastructure, Nigeria's institutional frameworks for data collection and management are inadequate. Government agencies, which should serve as key repositories and stewards of data, often operate in silos. Data is collected inconsistently, stored in inaccessible formats, and rarely shared across institutions. For example, statistics on public health, education, and agriculture\u2014critical for informed policymaking\u2014are frequently outdated or incomplete. The absence of a centralized, accessible data system not only hinders decision-making but also erodes public trust in government institutions.

Another significant challenge is the lack of standardization in data practices. While some sectors, such as telecommunications and banking, have made strides in adopting digital technologies and collecting reliable data, others lag far behind. In agriculture, which accounts for a significant portion of Nigeria's GDP, the use of data remains rudimentary. Farmers often rely on traditional methods and anecdotal evidence rather than leveraging modern tools like predictive analytics or geospatial data to optimize yields and reduce waste. This disparity in data adoption across sectors underscores the need for a coordinated national strategy to bridge the gap.

Despite these challenges, there are pockets of progress that offer hope. Nigeria's financial sector, driven by the rapid growth of fintech companies, has emerged as a leader in data utilization. Firms such as Paystack and Flutterwave have revolutionized payment systems, creating platforms that rely heavily on data to ensure seamless transactions, reduce fraud, and provide customer insights. These companies demonstrate how innovation and data can thrive even in the face of infrastructural and systemic challenges.

The technology ecosystem, centered in hubs like Lagos, Abuja, and Port Harcourt, is another bright spot. Startups and tech entrepreneurs are leveraging data to create solutions tailored to Nigeria's unique challenges. From health-tech platforms that connect patients to doctors via telemedicine to ed-tech companies providing digital learning resources, these innovators highlight the potential of data-driven approaches to transform key sectors. However, the impact of these initiatives remains limited by the broader systemic issues that permeate the national data landscape.

Education and data literacy represent another critical area of concern. For a country to harness the full potential of data, its citizens must possess the skills to interpret and utilize it effectively. In Nigeria, the education system has yet to fully integrate data science and related disciplines into its curriculum. While universities and private training institutes are beginning to offer programs in data analytics, these efforts remain nascent and insufficient to meet the growing demand for skilled professionals.

The lack of widespread data literacy hampers not only individual opportunities but also the ability of organizations and institutions to implement data-driven strategies.

The absence of clear data governance frameworks further complicates the situation. While Nigeria has made some progress in enacting laws related to cybersecurity and data protection\u2014such as the Nigeria Data Protection Regulation (NDPR)\u2014enforcement remains weak. Many organizations, particularly in the public sector, lack the capacity or willingness to comply with these regulations, leaving citizens' data vulnerable to breaches and misuse. Without robust governance structures, the potential benefits of a data-driven society will remain out of reach.

However, the challenges in Nigeria's data landscape are not insurmountable. The nation's growing population, youthful workforce, and expanding digital economy present significant opportunities to turn the tide. With strategic investments and a commitment to reform, Nigeria can build a data ecosystem that serves as a catalyst for growth and innovation.

To begin, the government must take a leadership role in creating a national data strategy. This strategy should prioritize the development of infrastructure, the standardization of data collection practices, and the establishment of centralized, open data repositories. By making data accessible to researchers, entrepreneurs, and policymakers, Nigeria can foster an environment of transparency and collaboration.

Additionally, partnerships between the public and private sectors are essential. The private sector has already demonstrated its ability to innovate with data, but these efforts need to be scaled through collaboration with government initiatives. For instance, telecom companies can play a crucial role in expanding internet access, while tech startups can help develop tools and platforms to address specific challenges in sectors such as agriculture and healthcare.

Education must also be a focal point of reform. Introducing data science into primary and secondary school curricula will ensure that the next generation is equipped with the skills needed to thrive in a data-driven world. Furthermore, vocational training programs and university partnerships with industry leaders can help bridge the gap for those already in the workforce.

Finally, strengthening data governance and privacy frameworks is critical to building public trust. Citizens need to feel confident that their data is being used ethically and securely. The government must enforce existing regulations and develop new policies that address emerging challenges, such as AI ethics and cross-border data flows.

Nigeria's current data landscape is a complex mix of challenges and opportunities. While the barriers to progress are significant, the potential rewards are far greater. By addressing infrastructural deficits, fostering innovation, and prioritizing education and governance, Nigeria can transform its data ecosystem and unlock new avenues for growth and development. As the nation takes its first steps toward becoming a data-driven society, the lessons learned from both local and global examples will be invaluable in shaping its future. This chapter has explored the present state of data in Nigeria, setting the stage for a deeper discussion of how data can serve as a catalyst for economic growth in the chapters to come.

2.1 Building an Inclusive Digital Infrastructure to Bridge Nigeria's Data Divide

A fundamental step toward transforming Nigeria's data landscape is addressing the digital divide that exists between urban and rural areas. The unequal distribution of internet access and digital tools exacerbates disparities in economic opportunities, education, and healthcare across the nation. For Nigeria to become a data-driven society, investments in inclusive digital infrastructure must be prioritized, aiming to create a cohesive framework that leaves no community behind.

Expanding broadband coverage to rural and underserved areas is critical for bridging the digital divide. Public-private partnerships can play a vital role in achieving this goal. Telecommunications companies can collaborate with the government to deploy affordable internet solutions tailored to rural communities. These partnerships could include incentives such as tax breaks for companies investing in rural connectivity and grants for deploying advanced technologies. Satellite internet technologies capable of bypassing the need for extensive ground infrastructure offer a practical solution for hard-to-reach areas. The use of micro-satellites ensures high-speed internet access, particularly for remote regions where traditional infrastructure is infeasible. Community-based wireless networks, operated by local cooperatives or supported by NGOs, can create sustainable models of connectivity tailored to the unique needs of each community. To accelerate progress, national initiatives focusing exclusively on bringing broadband access to areas with low penetration rates should be implemented. These initiatives could integrate mobile broadband expansion with efforts to improve digital literacy, ensuring communities can fully utilize the benefits of connectivity. For example, telecommunication companies could establish digital kiosks where locals can access internet services, participate in training sessions, and gain exposure to online tools.

Electrification initiatives must complement efforts to expand internet access. Without reliable power, digital technologies remain underutilized, and the maintenance of data centers becomes unsustainable. Renewable energy solutions such as solar-powered hubs, wind farms, and hybrid mini-grids could provide a dual benefit of enhancing energy access while supporting the digital infrastructure required for data collection and utilization. These renewable solutions can be tailored to local environments, creating long-term energy security for rural areas. Programs that combine electrification projects with internet deployment can ensure communities gain simultaneous access to energy and digital resources. Solar-powered internet hubs could serve as community technology centers, offering charging stations, Wi-Fi access, and digital training facilities. These hubs could also integrate healthcare and educational services, maximizing their impact on local development.

Access to digital devices is a cornerstone of digital inclusion. Initiatives like device subsidies, financing programs, and CSR-driven donations can enable low-income households to acquire smartphones, tablets, or computers. Collaborations between manufacturers, governments, and non-profits could produce affordable, durable devices designed specifically for low-resource settings. Ruggedized devices with extended battery life and offline capabilities could cater to areas with intermittent power and connectivity. Refurbishing and recycling programs for second-hand devices can further extend access. Through partnerships with tech companies, such programs could ensure older devices are restored and distributed to underserved populations, reducing e-waste while enhancing inclusivity.

The government must prioritize digital inclusivity by ensuring that all citizens, regardless of their location or socioeconomic status, can benefit from technological advancements. Targeted programs to train rural populations in digital skills and literacy will empower these communities to leverage data-driven opportunities, creating a more equitable and prosperous society. Mobile training units, equipped with laptops, projectors, and digital curricula, could travel to remote villages to deliver hands-on training. Instructors could teach participants to navigate the internet, use productivity software, and access digital platforms for healthcare, agriculture, and finance.

A digital inclusion initiative involving young volunteers trained in ICT could support these efforts, fostering a culture of mentorship and capacity-building at the grassroots level. Inclusivity should also extend to providing support for persons with disabilities. Adaptive technologies such as screen readers for the visually impaired and speech-to-text software for individuals with hearing impairments should be integrated into digital initiatives to ensure accessibility for all.

Big data holds immense potential to revolutionize Nigeria's approach to governance, economic planning, and social services. By harnessing large-scale datasets, Nigeria can gain valuable insights to drive evidence-based decision-making, improve service delivery, and tackle complex challenges.

In governance, big data can enhance transparency and accountability. Real-time data analytics could be used to track government spending, monitor the impact of social programs, and identify inefficiencies in public services. Imagine a platform where citizens can access dashboards showing detailed breakdowns of public spending, project timelines, and progress updates. Such systems not only deter corruption but also foster public trust by ensuring accountability. Big data applications in urban management can transform Nigeria's cities. Traffic congestion in metropolitan areas like Lagos could be alleviated by analyzing commuter data and optimizing infrastructure investments. Integrating big data with smart sensors could enable adaptive traffic signals that adjust to real-time congestion patterns, reducing delays and improving mobility.

In the agricultural sector, big data can revolutionize productivity and resilience. Predictive analytics can provide farmers with timely information about weather patterns, pest outbreaks, and optimal planting schedules. Platforms that aggregate satellite imagery, soil data, and market trends can deliver actionable insights to farmers via SMS or mobile apps. Digital platforms could connect farmers with buyers, input suppliers, and agricultural experts, reducing food waste and maximizing profit margins. Integrating big data into agricultural cooperatives promotes food security, increases rural incomes, and builds resilience against climate change.

In healthcare, big data can personalize healthcare delivery. Anonymized patient records could be analyzed to identify trends, such as rising rates of chronic illnesses, enabling targeted public health interventions. Mobile health platforms could leverage data to provide remote consultations, medication reminders, and tailored wellness plans, particularly in underserved areas. During pandemics, centralized dashboards could track infection hotspots, vaccination rates, and hospital capacities, guiding efficient responses. This integration fosters a resilient healthcare system capable of responding to emergencies while enhancing everyday care.

Big data has the potential to bolster national security. Analyzing data from diverse sources; social media, surveillance systems, and public reports allows security agencies to identify emerging threats and respond proactively. Predictive analytics could forecast areas at higher risk of conflict, enabling preemptive action. Geospatial data and modeling could guide disaster preparedness efforts, helping authorities identify high-risk areas for floods, fires, or droughts. Such capabilities protect lives while minimizing economic losses during crises.

To fully leverage big data, Nigeria must address challenges related to data storage, processing, and governance. Establishing regional data hubs with high-performance computing infrastructure decentralizes data management, ensuring faster and localized analytics. Training programs for data scientists and engineers should be prioritized, fostering a pipeline of talent to sustain big data initiatives. Collaboration with international organizations and tech giants introduces innovative technologies, enhancing Nigeria's ability to derive actionable insights from complex datasets.

Ensuring ethical and inclusive use of big data is paramount. Transparency in how data is collected, stored, and utilized builds public trust. Ethical frameworks must prioritize privacy and security while fostering innovation. By involving diverse stakeholders, government agencies, civil society, and marginalized groups, Nigeria can create a data ecosystem that is inclusive, equitable, and forward-looking.

CHAPTER 3
DATA AS A CATALYST FOR ECONOMIC GROWTH

Data is no longer a byproduct of economic activity; it is a driver of growth, innovation, and efficiency. Around the world, economies are being transformed by the intelligent use of data to optimize processes, identify opportunities, and enhance decision-making. For Nigeria, a nation with a youthful population and vast untapped resources, data holds the potential to unlock unprecedented economic progress. However, realizing this potential requires a deliberate and coordinated effort to integrate data into every aspect of the economy.

In Nigeria, one of the most critical sectors where data can drive growth is agriculture. Despite its significant contribution to GDP and employment, agriculture in Nigeria remains largely subsistence-based, with minimal use of technology and data analytics. Farmers often rely on traditional practices and lack access to vital information, such as weather forecasts, soil quality analysis, and market trends. By leveraging data, Nigeria can revolutionize its agricultural sector, enabling farmers to make informed decisions that boost productivity and reduce waste. Predictive analytics, for example, can help farmers anticipate crop diseases or determine the optimal time for planting and harvesting. Similarly, data on supply chains can reduce inefficiencies, ensuring that produce reaches markets quickly and at competitive prices.

Another sector ripe for transformation through data is financial services. Over the past decade, Nigeria's fintech ecosystem has emerged as a leader on the continent, with companies like Paystack, Flutterwave, and Interswitch driving innovation. These firms use data to analyze customer behavior, improve service delivery, and mitigate risks. For instance, machine learning algorithms can detect fraudulent transactions in real-time, protecting both businesses and consumers. The success of fintech in Nigeria highlights the broader potential of data to create new industries, enhance financial inclusion, and support small and medium enterprises (SMEs), which form the backbone of the economy. By extending credit to previously underserved populations through data-driven credit scoring models, fintech companies are enabling more Nigerians to participate in the formal economy.

Healthcare is another area where data can act as a catalyst for economic growth. A healthy population is the foundation of a productive workforce, and data has the power to transform healthcare delivery in Nigeria. Currently, the healthcare system is plagued by inefficiencies, from inadequate resource allocation to limited access to quality care in rural areas. By collecting and analyzing health data, Nigeria can identify disease patterns, allocate resources more effectively, and improve patient outcomes. For example, electronic health records can streamline the management of patient information, reducing redundancies and improving continuity of care. Additionally, data-driven public health campaigns can target specific communities with tailored interventions, reducing the spread of preventable diseases and lowering healthcare costs in the long term.

The energy sector also stands to benefit significantly from the integration of data. Nigeria's persistent electricity challenges are well-documented, with millions of citizens and businesses reliant on expensive and polluting generators. By using data to monitor and optimize energy distribution, Nigeria can improve efficiency and reduce waste. Smart grids, powered by real-time data, can predict demand fluctuations, prevent outages, and integrate renewable energy sources more effectively. Furthermore, data can play a role in expanding access to electricity by identifying underserved areas and guiding investments in infrastructure.

Education, too, holds immense potential for data-driven growth. A skilled and educated workforce is essential for a thriving economy, and data can help identify gaps in the education system and measure the effectiveness of interventions. By analyzing student performance data, policymakers can design targeted programs to address learning deficits, particularly in underserved communities. Additionally, data can help forecast future labor market needs, ensuring that educational institutions align their curricula with the demands of a rapidly changing economy. For example, as industries increasingly require expertise in fields like data science, artificial intelligence, and renewable energy, Nigeria's education system must adapt to prepare students for these emerging opportunities.

The potential of data extends beyond individual sectors to the broader economic environment. Macroeconomic planning, for instance, can be significantly enhanced by the use of reliable data. Accurate economic indicators, such as inflation rates, unemployment figures, and consumer spending patterns, are essential for effective policy formulation. Unfortunately, Nigeria has often struggled with inconsistent and outdated economic data, leading to suboptimal decision-making. By investing in data collection and analysis capabilities, the government can improve its ability to anticipate economic trends, respond to crises, and foster sustainable growth.

In the context of global trade, data can also enhance Nigeria's competitiveness. By analyzing trade patterns and market trends, Nigerian businesses can identify opportunities for export growth and diversify their revenue streams. For example, data on consumer preferences in international markets can guide the development of export-oriented products, while supply chain analytics can reduce costs and improve efficiency. Moreover, data-driven trade policies can help Nigeria negotiate more favorable agreements, ensuring that the nation benefits fully from its participation in global markets.

Despite its transformative potential, the integration of data into Nigeria's economy is not without challenges. Infrastructure deficits, as discussed in previous chapters, remain a significant barrier to progress. Additionally, there is a need for greater collaboration between the public and private sectors to build a cohesive data ecosystem. Trust is another critical issue; citizens and businesses must have confidence that their data will be used responsibly and ethically. Addressing these challenges requires not only technical solutions but also cultural and institutional changes that prioritize transparency, accountability, and inclusivity.

The economic potential of data for Nigeria is vast, but it will not be realized without deliberate effort. Policymakers must champion data as a strategic resource, creating an enabling environment for innovation and investment. At the same time, businesses and citizens must embrace a data-driven mindset, recognizing the value of information in driving progress. By integrating data into every aspect of the economy, Nigeria can unlock new opportunities for growth, enhance its global competitiveness, and improve the quality of life for its citizens. As we move to the next chapter, we will explore how data can transform governance, ensuring transparency, accountability, and efficiency in public administration.

2.1 Unlocking the Potential of Data-Driven Innovation in Nigeria's Technology Sector

The technology sector in Nigeria is uniquely positioned to serve as a hub of data-driven innovation, driving economic growth and fostering job creation. Startups and established tech firms alike have demonstrated how data can be used to create transformative solutions to some of the nation's most pressing challenges. However, the untapped potential of the sector suggests that much more can be achieved with the right support systems, targeted policies, and sustainable strategies for growth.

Tech hubs like Yaba in Lagos, often referred to as "Yabacon Valley," serve as incubators for data-driven enterprises. These hubs are fostering a new generation of entrepreneurs who are developing apps, platforms, and software solutions that rely on data analytics to deliver value. For example, data is being used to power applications in ride-hailing, e-commerce, and logistics, sectors that are rapidly growing in Nigeria's urban centers. Ride-hailing apps like Bolt and Uber rely on geospatial data and real-time traffic analytics to optimize routes and reduce waiting times for riders, while e-commerce platforms like Jumia use data to recommend personalized products, manage inventory, and predict consumer behavior. These advancements have reshaped urban economies, creating jobs, enhancing convenience, and increasing market efficiency.

Expanding these solutions to rural areas, however, requires deliberate investment in infrastructure and capacity-building initiatives. For example, rural communities often lack the reliable internet connectivity necessary to support such platforms. Introducing affordable internet solutions through public-private partnerships and deploying mobile networks tailored to the unique challenges of rural geographies can bridge this gap. Moreover, training programs can empower local entrepreneurs to adopt and adapt these technologies for their specific needs, ensuring that innovation is inclusive and far-reaching. Governments and NGOs can facilitate this expansion by offering grants and resources to tech startups willing to operate in less-served regions, creating a win-win scenario for businesses and communities.

The growth of artificial intelligence (AI) and machine learning in Nigeria's tech sector presents significant opportunities for innovation. AI-powered solutions can analyze vast datasets to optimize business operations, predict market trends, and create personalized customer experiences. For instance, AI is already being used in Nigeria's banking sector to improve customer service through chatbots, enhance fraud detection systems, and develop predictive financial models. Expanding these technologies to other industries, such as manufacturing and tourism, can unlock new revenue streams and enhance global competitiveness. AI-based analytics could revolutionize Nigeria's manufacturing industry by identifying inefficiencies in production lines, predicting equipment failures before they occur, and reducing overall operational costs.

In agriculture, AI systems could analyze environmental data to recommend optimal planting schedules, helping farmers mitigate risks associated with unpredictable weather patterns and climate change. The hospitality and tourism sector, meanwhile, could leverage AI to develop personalized travel experiences, offering tourists curated itineraries based on their preferences and real-time local data. The potential for AI applications in Nigeria is vast, but fully harnessing this technology requires significant investments in infrastructure, training, and policy development.

However, realizing the full potential of the tech sector requires addressing critical challenges, including funding gaps, talent shortages, and policy constraints. While venture capital investment in Nigerian startups has grown significantly in recent years, many promising companies still struggle to access the financial resources needed to scale their operations. Public and private sector partnerships can establish innovation funds or grants to provide startups with the capital they need to advance. Additionally, creating platforms for venture capitalists and angel investors to connect with tech entrepreneurs can foster greater financial support for the sector. Partnerships with international tech companies and financial institutions can bring not only funding but also expertise, allowing Nigerian startups to learn from global best practices.

The demand for skilled data scientists, software developers, and engineers far outpaces the supply, highlighting the need for targeted educational reforms and workforce development programs.

Institutions of higher learning should collaborate with industry stakeholders to align curricula with the needs of the technology sector. Initiatives such as coding boot camps, internships, and tech incubators can help bridge the talent gap, equipping young Nigerians with the skills required to thrive in a digital economy. Furthermore, early exposure to technology and data literacy in primary and secondary education can cultivate interest and aptitude among young learners, ensuring a continuous pipeline of talent for the future.

Mentorship programs connecting experienced professionals with budding entrepreneurs can further accelerate the transfer of knowledge and expertise. These programs can be particularly effective in demystifying advanced technologies like AI, blockchain, and the Internet of Things (IoT), enabling entrepreneurs to integrate innovative tools into their business models. By fostering a supportive ecosystem for tech innovation, Nigeria can not only boost its economy but also position itself as a leader in Africa's digital transformation.

Strategic partnerships with global tech firms, coupled with government incentives for research and development, can accelerate.

progress in this vital sector. Tax breaks for companies investing in local tech hubs, along with policies promoting data sharing and innovation, can create an environment conducive to sustained growth. Additionally, government-backed programs to certify and support tech startups can increase investor confidence, opening doors to larger funding opportunities.

2.2 Creating a Data-Enabled Environment for Small and Medium Enterprises (SMEs)

Small and Medium Enterprises (SMEs) form the backbone of Nigeria's economy, contributing significantly to employment and GDP. Yet, many of these businesses operate in isolation, lacking access to the data they need to grow and thrive. Empowering SMEs with data-driven tools and insights can be a significant change, enabling them to compete more effectively in local and global markets.

One of the key challenges SMEs faces is limited access to market intelligence. Many small businesses lack the resources to conduct market research, leaving them unaware of consumer trends, pricing strategies, and competitive dynamics. By establishing centralized platforms that aggregate and share market data, the government and private sector can provide SMEs with actionable insights to guide their decision-making. For example, a national SME data platform could collate information on consumer preferences, industry benchmarks, and pricing trends, offering businesses an invaluable resource for strategic planning.

Additionally, digital payment systems and customer relationship management (CRM) platforms powered by data analytics can help SMEs improve operational efficiency and customer engagement.

Data tools that track sales patterns, customer preferences, and seasonal demand enable businesses to tailor their offerings and enhance customer loyalty. For instance, a retail business could use data analytics to determine which products are most popular in specific locations, ensuring inventory is stocked accordingly. CRM platforms can also segment customer data, allowing SMEs to launch targeted marketing campaigns and improve retention rates. These technologies not only enhance profitability but also foster stronger relationships with customers, providing a competitive edge.

Data also plays a crucial role in expanding access to credit for SMEs. Traditional banks often perceive small businesses as high-risk borrowers due to limited financial histories. However, alternative credit scoring models that leverage data from digital transactions, utility payments, and social media activity can provide a more accurate assessment of creditworthiness. Fintech companies in Nigeria are already pioneering these approaches, creating micro-loan products that cater to underserved entrepreneurs. Scaling these innovations requires greater collaboration with traditional financial institutions and regulatory support to ensure fair lending practices and expand reach.

Integrating SMEs into the broader digital economy is essential for long-term growth. E-commerce platforms, for instance, can serve as gateways for SMEs to reach wider markets, both domestically and internationally. These platforms enable small businesses to showcase their products to a larger audience, process transactions securely, and access logistics solutions for delivery. Initiatives aimed at reducing barriers to entry, such as subsidizing fees for platform usage or providing free onboarding services, can accelerate SME participation in digital commerce.

To foster a data-enabled environment for SMEs, targeted government policies are needed to support innovation and capacity building. Establishing SME-focused tech hubs in regional areas could provide small businesses with access to data tools, mentorship, and training programs. Partnerships with multinational corporations can also bring global best practices to Nigerian SMEs, offering technical expertise and resources. Programs that encourage cross-border collaboration could open new opportunities for SMEs to expand into international markets, driving export growth and economic diversification.

In conclusion, the integration of data-driven practices across Nigeria's economy offers immense potential to unlock new opportunities, foster innovation, and enhance productivity. By supporting the technology sector and empowering SMEs, data stands as a critical enabler of progress. As Nigeria continues its journey toward becoming a data-driven society, these strategic interventions will ensure that the benefits of the digital revolution are felt across all segments of the economy. With sustained effort, Nigeria can achieve its vision of a data-driven future, fostering inclusivity, growth, and resilience.

CHAPTER 4
BUILDING A DATA-DRIVEN GOVERNMENT

Effective governance is the foundation of any successful society, and in the modern era, data has become a critical tool for achieving transparency, accountability, and efficiency in public administration. Around the world, governments are leveraging data to streamline operations, improve service delivery, and engage citizens. For Nigeria, where governance challenges such as corruption, inefficiency, and lack of transparency have long hindered progress, the adoption of data-driven approaches offers a pathway to transformative change.

One of the most significant ways data can enhance governance is by enabling evidence-based decision-making. Traditionally, many policy decisions in Nigeria have been made based on intuition or political expediency rather than robust analysis. This approach often leads to suboptimal outcomes, such as misallocated resources, ineffective programs, and missed opportunities. By integrating data into the policymaking process, Nigeria can shift from reactive governance to proactive governance. For example, real-time data on population demographics, economic activity, and infrastructure needs can help policymakers anticipate challenges and design targeted interventions. Whether it is planning new schools, allocating healthcare resources, or investing in transportation networks, data ensures that decisions are guided by facts rather than guesswork.

Data also plays a crucial role in enhancing transparency and combating corruption, which has been a persistent issue in Nigeria's public sector. By digitizing government operations and creating open data platforms, Nigeria can reduce opportunities for fraud and increase accountability. For instance, digital payment systems can eliminate the need for intermediaries, reducing the risk of embezzlement or mismanagement of funds. Similarly, open procurement systems, where data on government contracts is publicly available, can deter favoritism and ensure fair competition. Citizens, journalists, and civil society organizations can use this data to hold government officials accountable, fostering a culture of transparency and trust.

Another area where data can drive significant improvements is in public service delivery. Across sectors such as healthcare, education, and social welfare, inefficiencies often arise from a lack of accurate information about citizens' needs. By building robust data systems, the government can better understand and respond to these needs. For example, a centralized health database could track disease outbreaks in real-time, enabling faster and more effective responses. Similarly, data on school enrollment and performance could inform education policies, ensuring that resources are directed to areas with the greatest need. By aligning services with demand, data-driven governance can improve the quality of life for citizens while maximizing the impact of public spending.

Census and population data are particularly critical for effective governance in Nigeria, yet the country has struggled to conduct reliable and timely censuses. Accurate population data is essential for everything from electoral planning to infrastructure development. Without it, the government risks making decisions based on outdated or incomplete information, perpetuating inefficiencies, and inequalities. Investing in modern data collection methods, such as geospatial mapping and digital surveys, can address these gaps and provide a solid foundation for evidence-based governance.

In addition to improving internal processes, data can enhance citizen engagement and participation in governance. In a democratic society, public trust in government is built on transparency, inclusivity, and accountability. Data-driven tools, such as mobile apps and online platforms, can empower citizens to provide feedback, report issues, and track the progress of government initiatives. For example, a citizen could use a mobile app to report potholes, broken streetlights, or other infrastructure problems, with the data automatically routed to the relevant authorities for action. These platforms not only improve service delivery but also strengthen the relationship between citizens and the government, fostering a sense of shared responsibility.

The use of data in governance also extends to election management, a critical area for Nigeria's democracy. Transparent and credible elections are the cornerstone of democratic governance, yet electoral processes in Nigeria have often been marred by irregularities and controversies. Data can enhance the integrity of elections by improving voter registration, monitoring turnout, and detecting irregularities. Biometric voter identification systems, for instance, can prevent double voting and ensure that elections are conducted fairly. Additionally, data analytics can help identify patterns of voter suppression or manipulation, enabling swift corrective action.

While the benefits of data-driven governance are clear, implementing such systems in Nigeria is not without challenges. One major obstacle is the lack of capacity and expertise within government institutions. Many agencies lack the technical skills and infrastructure needed to collect, analyze, and utilize data effectively. Training programs and partnerships with private sector organizations and international donors can help bridge this gap, building the technical capacity required for data-driven governance.

Another challenge is the issue of data security and privacy. As the government collects and stores more data, ensuring its protection becomes critical. Breaches or misuse of sensitive information can undermine public trust and have far-reaching consequences. Nigeria must establish robust data protection frameworks, drawing on global best practices to safeguard citizens' information. The Nigeria Data Protection Regulation (NDPR) is a step in the right direction, but it must be enforced consistently and complemented by broader legislation that addresses emerging threats.

To overcome these challenges, Nigeria must adopt a phased approach to building a data-driven government. This process should begin with pilot projects in key sectors, allowing for experimentation and refinement before scaling up. For instance, the government could start by digitizing one aspect of healthcare delivery, such as vaccine distribution, and use the lessons learned to inform broader initiatives. By demonstrating the tangible benefits of data-driven approaches, these pilots can build momentum and secure buy-in from stakeholders across the public and private sectors.

In the long term, building a data-driven government will require a cultural shift within Nigeria's public sector. Policymakers, civil servants, and citizens must recognize the value of data and embrace its use as a tool for progress. This shift will not happen overnight, but with sustained effort and leadership, it is achievable.

Data has the power to transform governance in Nigeria, making it more transparent, efficient, and responsive to the needs of citizens. By integrating data into decision-making, service delivery, and citizen engagement, the government can build a foundation for sustainable development and inclusive growth. As Nigeria moves toward a data-driven future, the lessons learned in governance will provide a model for other sectors, reinforcing the idea that data is not just a tool but a catalyst for national transformation. In the next chapter, we will explore how data can empower Nigeria's entrepreneurs, driving innovation and economic diversification.

4.1 Enhancing Local Governance Through Data Integration

While data-driven governance often focuses on national-level initiatives, the potential impact at the local government level in Nigeria is equally profound. Local governments serve as the closest link between citizens and public administration, yet they often face the most significant challenges in terms of capacity, transparency, and resource allocation. Integrating data into local governance can transform these challenges into opportunities, empowering local authorities to deliver better services, manage resources more effectively, and engage with their communities in meaningful ways.

Resource management is one of the most critical areas where data can make a difference. Local governments often grapple with inadequate budgets and limited information about their constituencies' needs, leading to inefficient use of scarce resources. Data-driven approaches enable them to make informed decisions about resource allocation, ensuring maximum impact. For example, geospatial data can help map underserved areas in need of critical infrastructure such as roads, water supply, or healthcare facilities. By layering demographic data onto these maps, local governments can also identify vulnerable populations and tailor their interventions accordingly. A town experiencing rapid population growth may prioritize new housing projects or expand public transportation networks, while a community with aging infrastructure might focus on renovations and maintenance.

Transparency and accountability are perennial issues in local governance. Corruption and mismanagement in local councils erode public trust, hinder development, and exacerbate inequality. By digitizing financial records, procurement processes, and service delivery metrics, local governments can create open data platforms accessible to citizens. These platforms allow residents to track how funds are allocated and monitor the progress of local projects, fostering a culture of accountability. For instance, a digital dashboard could display the status of a road construction project, from budget allocation to completion timelines, offering real-time updates that deter malpractices and empower citizens to hold officials accountable. Over time, such transparency initiatives build trust between communities and their local governments, enhancing civic engagement and collaboration.

Engaging with constituents is another area where data can revolutionize local governance. Digital tools such as mobile apps, SMS platforms, and interactive dashboards can facilitate two-way communication between citizens and local authorities. Residents can report issues such as waste collection delays, potholes, or broken streetlights directly to the relevant departments, while authorities can use analytics to identify recurring problems or trends. For example, if a particular neighborhood consistently reports power outages, the data can prompt a deeper investigation into the root causes, leading to more sustainable solutions. Additionally, these platforms can disseminate information about local initiatives, town hall meetings, or emergency alerts, ensuring that citizens remain informed and engaged.

Implementing these changes requires significant investment in infrastructure and capacity-building. Local governments often lack the technical expertise and financial resources needed to establish data-driven systems. Partnerships with state and federal agencies, as well as collaboration with private sector organizations and NGOs, can provide the necessary support. For example, tech companies could assist in developing user-friendly apps and platforms, while international development organizations might fund pilot programs to demonstrate the benefits of data integration. These pilot programs could serve as a model for broader adoption, showcasing how data-driven local governance leads to tangible improvements in service delivery and community well-being.

Training personnel is another critical component of this transformation. Local government staff must be equipped with the skills to collect, analyze, and interpret data effectively. Workshops, online courses, and mentorship programs can help build this capacity, ensuring that data is used responsibly and strategically. Additionally, fostering a culture of innovation within local governments can encourage the adoption of new technologies and practices, further enhancing their ability to serve their communities.

4. 2 Data-Driven Crisis Management and Emergency Response

Nigeria is no stranger to crises, from natural disasters such as floods and droughts to human-caused challenges like insurgency and public health emergencies. Data has the potential to revolutionize how the government prepares for, responds to, and recovers from these events, saving lives and minimizing economic losses. By leveraging data at every stage of crisis management, Nigeria can enhance its resilience and capacity to navigate complex challenges.

One of the most critical applications of data in crisis management is early warning systems. By analyzing historical data, weather patterns, and real-time monitoring, the government can predict natural disasters such as floods or droughts and issue timely alerts to vulnerable communities. For instance, flood-prone regions can be equipped with sensors that provide data on rising water levels, triggering evacuation plans before disaster strikes. Satellite imagery can also play a pivotal role in identifying deforestation and desertification trends, guiding policies to address these long-term environmental risks. Early detection not only saves lives but also reduces the economic costs associated with disaster response and recovery.

During emergencies, data facilitates the efficient allocation of resources. Real-time information about affected populations, available infrastructure, and supply chain logistics allows authorities to deploy relief efforts where they are needed most. For example, during the COVID-19 pandemic, countries that used data to track infection rates, hospital capacity, and vaccination progress were able to manage healthcare resources more effectively, reducing fatalities and improving outcomes. Nigeria can adopt similar approaches for future public health crises, leveraging electronic health records, mobile health apps, and community-based reporting systems to coordinate responses. These tools enable health officials to identify hotspots, allocate medical supplies, and ensure equitable access to care.

Post-crisis recovery also benefits significantly from data-driven strategies. Damage assessments can be conducted using drone technology and satellite imagery, providing accurate and timely information for reconstruction efforts. This data can inform decisions about where to rebuild infrastructure, how to allocate resources, and which communities require the most urgent attention. Additionally, data on displaced populations can guide the design of resettlement programs, ensuring that housing, education, and employment opportunities are distributed equitably.

To build a robust data-driven crisis management system, Nigeria must invest in the necessary infrastructure and capacity. Establishing data-sharing frameworks between government agencies, training personnel in data analysis and interpretation, and integrating advanced technologies such as AI and machine learning are essential steps. For instance, machine learning algorithms can analyze vast datasets to predict the likelihood of specific crises, enabling preemptive action. Collaboration with international organizations and research institutions can also provide access to expertise, tools, and funding for disaster preparedness initiatives.

Moreover, public engagement is a crucial element of data-driven crisis management. Educating communities about how to interpret and act on early warnings can significantly improve response times and reduce casualties. Awareness campaigns, community drills, and accessible information platforms can empower citizens to play an active role in their safety. For example, mobile apps that send localized alerts about impending disasters, coupled with guidance on evacuation routes and safe shelters, can save countless lives.

By adopting data-driven approaches to crisis management, Nigeria can not only protect lives and property but also strengthen public trust in the government's ability to respond effectively to challenges. These strategies position the country to adapt to a rapidly changing world, addressing both immediate crises and long-term risks. As data becomes an integral part of governance at all levels, Nigeria will be better equipped to build a more resilient, inclusive, and sustainable future.

CHAPTER 5
DATA AND THE NIGERIAN ENTREPRENEUR

Entrepreneurship has long been heralded as the engine of economic growth, and in Nigeria, it holds the promise of creating jobs, driving innovation, and reducing poverty. With one of the youngest populations in the world, Nigeria is home to millions of aspiring entrepreneurs eager to solve local challenges and build businesses that can compete globally. However, the success of entrepreneurship in the modern era increasingly depends on the availability and effective use of data. For Nigerian entrepreneurs, data is not just a tool; it is a competitive advantage that can unlock opportunities, optimize operations, and transform visions into reality.

One of the most significant ways data empowers entrepreneurs is by providing insights into market trends and customer behavior. In Nigeria, where consumer preferences can vary significantly across regions, data allows businesses to tailor their products and services to meet the specific needs of their target audience. For example, an entrepreneur launching a fashion brand in Lagos might analyze data on purchasing patterns, popular styles, and social media trends to design collections that resonate with their customers. Similarly, a tech startup developing a mobile app for rural farmers could use data to identify the most common challenges faced by their users, such as access to weather forecasts or market prices, and design solutions accordingly.

Data also plays a critical role in helping entrepreneurs optimize their operations and reduce costs. For small and medium-sized enterprises (SMEs), which often operate on tight budgets, even minor inefficiencies can have a significant impact on profitability. By analyzing operational data, businesses can identify bottlenecks, streamline processes, and allocate resources more effectively. For instance, a logistics company might use data to map the fastest delivery routes, reducing fuel costs and improving customer satisfaction. Similarly, a retail business could analyze sales data to identify slow-moving inventory and adjust its purchasing strategy to minimize waste.

Access to data is particularly crucial for Nigerian entrepreneurs seeking to secure funding. Investors are increasingly looking for data-driven insights to assess the viability of a business. Startups that can demonstrate a deep understanding of their market, backed by solid data, are more likely to attract investment. Financial metrics, customer acquisition rates, and growth projections, all derived from data, provide investors with the confidence that a business is well-positioned for success. Moreover, data can help entrepreneurs identify the most suitable funding sources, whether it is venturing capital, grants, or crowdfunding platforms, and tailoring their pitches to meet the expectations of potential investors.

In addition to its operational benefits, data fosters innovation by inspiring new business ideas and enabling entrepreneurs to address unmet needs. Nigeria's vibrant tech ecosystem is a testament to the power of data-driven innovation. From fintech platforms that provide access to financial services for the unbanked to health-tech solutions that connect patients with doctors in underserved areas, data is driving the creation of products and services that transform lives. For example, startups like PiggyVest and Cowrywise have leveraged data to develop savings and investment platforms that cater to Nigeria's growing middle class. By analyzing user behavior and financial trends, these companies have created intuitive tools that empower Nigerians to take control of their finances.

Despite its potential, the integration of data into entrepreneurship in Nigeria faces significant challenges. One of the primary barriers is the limited availability of reliable and accessible data. Many entrepreneurs struggle to find the information they need to make informed decisions, as public and private data sources are often fragmented or outdated. For example, market research reports and industry statistics, which are readily available in more developed economies, are often scarce or prohibitively expensive in Nigeria. This lack of access to data puts Nigerian entrepreneurs at a disadvantage, forcing them to rely on anecdotal evidence or guesswork.

Another challenge is the lack of data literacy among entrepreneurs. While many business owners recognize the importance of data, they often lack the skills to analyze and interpret it effectively. This skills gap is particularly pronounced among smaller businesses that cannot afford to hire data analysts or invest in advanced tools. Bridging this gap requires targeted training programs and the development of affordable, user-friendly data platforms tailored to the needs of Nigerian entrepreneurs.

To address these challenges and fully harness the power of data, Nigeria must build a robust ecosystem that supports data-driven entrepreneurship. This effort begins with improving access to data. Public agencies, private organizations, and academic institutions must collaborate to create centralized data repositories that are easily accessible to entrepreneurs. Open data initiatives, where government and corporate data are made available to the public, can play a critical role in this process. For example, anonymized data on consumer spending patterns, transportation networks, or agricultural production could provide valuable insights for businesses across various sectors.

Education and capacity-building are equally important. Entrepreneurship programs should integrate data literacy into their curricula, teaching aspiring business owners how to collect, analyze, and apply data in their decision-making processes. Additionally, mentorship programs that pair entrepreneurs with data-savvy professionals can provide hands-on guidance and foster a culture of data-driven innovation.

The private sector also has a crucial role to play in supporting data-driven entrepreneurship. Tech companies, in particular, can develop tools and platforms that make it easier for small businesses to leverage data. For instance, cloud-based analytics tools that offer affordable subscription models can help entrepreneurs access the power of data without significant upfront investment. Furthermore, partnerships between startups and larger corporations can facilitate knowledge transfer and provide access to resources that smaller businesses might not otherwise have.

Finally, the government must create an enabling environment for data-driven entrepreneurship. This includes enacting policies that promote data sharing, protecting intellectual property rights, and encouraging investment in the tech sector. By providing grants and incentives for data-driven startups, the government can accelerate the growth of businesses that drive economic diversification and job creation.

Data is a significant change for Nigerian entrepreneurs, offering the tools they need to innovate, compete, and grow. By addressing the barriers to data access and literacy, Nigeria can unlock the full potential of its entrepreneurial ecosystem, fostering a new generation of businesses that drive economic transformation. As we move to the next chapter, we will examine the obstacles that stand in the way of Nigeria's data revolution and explore strategies for overcoming them.

5.1 Building Data-Driven Marketplaces: The Role of Digital Platforms

Digital marketplaces powered by data are transforming commerce across the globe, and for Nigerian entrepreneurs, these platforms represent a significant opportunity to access larger markets and compete on a global scale. By aggregating data on buyers, sellers, preferences, and transaction patterns, digital marketplaces provide an efficient and scalable way for businesses to reach their target audiences and optimize their operations. As the global economy increasingly leans on digital platforms for commerce, the growth and accessibility of data-driven marketplaces in Nigeria are set to redefine the entrepreneurial landscape.

E-commerce platforms like Jumia and Konga have already made strides in this space, offering Nigerian entrepreneurs a digital storefront to showcase their products. These platforms leverage sophisticated data analytics to enhance user experiences by recommending products to customers based on their browsing and purchasing histories. For entrepreneurs, this means increased visibility and higher conversion rates, as their offerings are matched with potential buyers more effectively. Additionally, these platforms provide vital insights into customer behavior, preferences, and market trends, enabling businesses to refine their strategies and align their offerings with demand.

Beyond traditional e-commerce, niche marketplaces tailored to specific industries can provide even greater value. For example, platforms focused on agriculture can connect farmers with buyers, input suppliers, and financial services, streamlining the supply chain and reducing inefficiencies. Agricultural marketplaces can employ data analytics to predict market demand, guide pricing strategies, and improve distribution logistics. For instance, farmers could use real-time data on weather conditions and market prices to determine the optimal timing for planting, harvesting, and selling their crops. Similarly, artisan-focused platforms could connect craftspeople to international buyers, boosting exports and preserving cultural heritage through digital channels.

However, the success of data-driven marketplaces depends on the availability of reliable data and infrastructure. Entrepreneurs need tools to track their sales, manage inventory, and analyze customer feedback in real time. Cloud-based software solutions and mobile-friendly interfaces can make these capabilities accessible to small business owners who may lack advanced technical expertise. For example, simple mobile apps designed to record transactions and track inventory can empower small-scale vendors to operate more efficiently and scale their operations. These tools can also integrate seamlessly with payment gateways, providing end-to-end solutions that simplify business operations.

Collaborations between digital platforms and government or private-sector partners can further enhance these marketplaces. For instance, partnerships with logistics companies can improve delivery networks, ensuring that products reach customers promptly and cost-effectively. Collaborations with financial institutions can offer integrated payment solutions, access to credit, and microfinancing options tailored to small businesses. For example, e-commerce platforms could introduce Buy Now, Pay Later (BNPL) schemes, enabling customers to purchase products while improving cash flow for sellers. Government involvement, such as subsidizing internet costs or offering grants to digital platforms that prioritize local entrepreneurs, can further accelerate marketplace adoption and growth.

Moreover, building trust and confidence in digital marketplaces is essential for their success. Many Nigerians remain wary of online transactions due to concerns about fraud and data security. Strengthening cybersecurity measures, offering transparent refund policies, and implementing robust seller verification processes are critical to fostering trust. Educational campaigns and training programs can also help entrepreneurs and customers navigate digital platforms safely and effectively, expanding participation in the digital economy.

By creating a supportive ecosystem for digital marketplaces, Nigeria can empower its entrepreneurs to thrive in the digital economy. The development of such ecosystems will not only increase local economic activity but also enable Nigerian businesses to compete globally, showcasing their products and services to international markets. As these platforms evolve, they will drive innovation, create jobs, and contribute significantly to the nation's economic diversification efforts.

5.2 Harnessing Data for Social Impact Entrepreneurship

Data-driven approaches are not just transforming profit-driven enterprises; they are also revolutionizing social impact entrepreneurship in Nigeria. Social enterprises, which aim to address pressing societal challenges while maintaining financial sustainability, can leverage data to scale their impact and achieve their goals more effectively. The intersection of data and social entrepreneurship represents a powerful avenue for tackling systemic issues in healthcare, education, environmental sustainability, and community development.

Health-tech startups focused on improving access to medical care in underserved communities can use data to identify gaps in healthcare delivery and tailor their solutions accordingly. By analyzing data on disease prevalence, patient demographics, and resource availability, these startups can deploy mobile clinics, telemedicine platforms, and preventive care programs where they are needed most. For instance, a telemedicine app could use patient data to prioritize consultations for high-risk individuals, ensuring timely intervention. Health-tech platforms can also aggregate anonymized data to inform public health policies, enabling targeted responses to health crises such as epidemics or maternal health challenges.

Similarly, education-focused social enterprises can use data to monitor student performance, track attendance, and evaluate the effectiveness of learning interventions. Platforms like uLesson, which provides digital learning resources, rely on data to personalize content for students and identify areas where additional support is required. Advanced analytics can help educators pinpoint systemic challenges, such as low literacy rates in specific regions, and design targeted programs to address these issues. Furthermore, data-driven insights can inform decisions about curriculum development, teacher training, and resource allocation, ensuring that educational initiatives are impactful and inclusive.

Environmental sustainability initiatives are another area where data is driving innovation. Startups working on renewable energy, waste management, and climate resilience can use data to optimize their operations and measure their environmental impact. For example, solar energy companies can use predictive analytics to anticipate energy demand and optimize the placement of solar panels, maximizing efficiency and minimizing costs. Waste recycling enterprises can employ geospatial data to map collection routes, reducing fuel consumption and increasing recycling rates. Additionally, climate-focused social enterprises can leverage weather and environmental data to develop tools that help communities adapt to the effects of climate change, such as early warning systems for floods or droughts.

To support social impact entrepreneurs, Nigeria needs to develop an ecosystem that combines data access, funding, and mentorship. Open data initiatives can provide social enterprises with the information they need to innovate, while partnerships with academic institutions can foster research and development in areas such as public health and sustainability. Impact investors and philanthropic organizations can play a crucial role by providing financial support and expertise to data-driven social enterprises. For example, an impact fund targeting health-tech startups could offer seed capital, while mentorship programs could connect social entrepreneurs with industry veterans who can guide their growth.

Government policies that incentivize social entrepreneurship are also essential for fostering innovation. Tax breaks, grants, and subsidies for social enterprises working in priority areas such as education, healthcare, and the environment can encourage more entrepreneurs to enter these fields. Additionally, the establishment of innovation hubs focused on social impact can create spaces for collaboration, knowledge sharing, and experimentation.

Building public awareness and trust is another key component of fostering social entrepreneurship. Many Nigerians remain unaware of the potential benefits of data-driven social enterprises, and outreach campaigns can help highlight success stories, demonstrating how these initiatives address pressing societal challenges. By showcasing the tangible benefits of social impact entrepreneurship, these campaigns can inspire more individuals to join the movement and contribute to the nation's development.

By fostering data-driven social entrepreneurship, Nigeria can tackle complex challenges in healthcare, education, and the environment, creating a more equitable and sustainable future. Entrepreneurs who combine business acumen with a commitment to social impact will not only drive economic growth but also contribute to the broader development of society. As these initiatives scale, they will demonstrate the transformative power of data in addressing systemic issues, reinforcing Nigeria's position as a leader in innovation and social progress.

CHAPTER 6
OVERCOMING BARRIERS TO DATA UTILIZATION

The promise of a data-driven Nigeria is immense, but realizing this vision requires addressing a series of entrenched barriers that hinder the effective use of data. From infrastructural deficits to cultural attitudes, these challenges are multi-dimensional, touching every aspect of society. However, by understanding these obstacles, Nigeria can develop targeted strategies to overcome them and unlock the full potential of its data ecosystem.

One of the most pressing barriers to data utilization in Nigeria is inadequate infrastructure. Reliable access to electricity and internet connectivity remains a persistent challenge across much of the country, particularly in rural areas. Data centers, which serve as the backbone of a modern data ecosystem, require consistent power and high-speed connectivity to function effectively. Without these basic prerequisites, efforts to build robust data systems are severely limited. In urban centers like Lagos and Abuja, progress is being made, with private companies investing in broadband networks and renewable energy solutions. However, these developments have yet to reach much of the population, creating a digital divide that limits equitable access to data-driven opportunities.

Another significant challenge is the lack of centralized and accessible data repositories. In many cases, data collected by government agencies and private organizations is stored in silos, fragmented across different platforms and formats. This fragmentation makes it difficult for researchers, policymakers, and businesses to access the information they need. For instance, a health-tech startup trying to develop solutions for rural clinics might struggle to find up-to-date data on disease prevalence or patient demographics. Similarly, policymakers working on agricultural reforms might lack accurate statistics on crop production or market prices. Without reliable and accessible data, decision-making becomes a guessing game, undermining efforts to address critical issues.

Data literacy is another critical barrier. While the concept of data-driven decision-making is gaining traction, many Nigerians still lack the skills needed to collect, analyze, and interpret data effectively. This skills gap is particularly pronounced among small and medium-sized enterprises (SMEs) and public sector workers, who often rely on outdated methods of record-keeping and analysis. Even when data is available, it is often underutilized because individuals and organizations lack the capacity to extract meaningful insights. Bridging this gap requires a concerted effort to integrate data education into school curricula, provide professional training programs, and promote a culture of lifelong learning.

Cultural attitudes toward data also present a challenge. In some cases, there is resistance to adopting data-driven approaches due to mistrust or fear of change. This resistance can be found at all levels of society, from individuals hesitant to share personal information to institutions wary of transparency. For example, some businesses may view data collection as an unnecessary expense rather than an investment, while government agencies might be reluctant to publish data that could expose inefficiencies or corruption. Changing these attitudes requires a shift in mindset, emphasizing the value of data as a tool for empowerment rather than a threat.

Privacy and security concerns further complicate the adoption of data-driven systems. As more data is collected and stored, the risk of breaches and misuse increases. In Nigeria, incidents of cybercrime and data leaks have highlighted vulnerabilities in existing systems, eroding public trust. Citizens are understandably wary of sharing their personal information if they feel it might be used against them or fall into the wrong hands. Addressing these concerns requires robust data protection frameworks and transparent practices that prioritize ethical data usage. The Nigeria Data Protection Regulation (NDPR) is a step in the right direction, but enforcement must be strengthened to ensure compliance across all sectors.

Another barrier is the lack of investment in data infrastructure and technology. While the private sector has made strides in areas like fintech and e-commerce, public sector investment in data systems remains limited. Budget constraints and competing priorities often push data projects to the backburner, leaving critical gaps in areas like healthcare, education, and agriculture. To address this, Nigeria must prioritize data as a strategic asset, allocating resources to build the infrastructure and systems needed to support a data-driven economy. Partnerships with international organizations, development agencies, and private investors can also provide the funding and expertise required to accelerate progress.

Despite these challenges, there are clear strategies for overcoming the barriers to data utilization in Nigeria. Primarily, the government must take the lead in building a cohesive and accessible data ecosystem. This involves creating centralized data repositories that consolidate information from various sources and make it available to stakeholders in a standardized format. Open data initiatives, where anonymized datasets are shared publicly, can foster collaboration and innovation across sectors.

Education and capacity-building are also essential. Integrating data literacy into primary and secondary school curricula will ensure that future generations are equipped with the skills they need to thrive in a data-driven world. At the same time, professional training programs and public awareness campaigns can help bridge the skills gap for those already in the workforce. By promoting a culture of data literacy, Nigeria can empower individuals and organizations to make informed decisions and drive progress.

To address infrastructural challenges, Nigeria must invest in expanding internet connectivity and reliable power supply, particularly in underserved areas. Public-private partnerships can play a key role in this effort, with telecom companies, energy providers, and tech firms working together to build the necessary infrastructure. For example, initiatives like community-based solar energy projects and mobile broadband networks can bring connectivity and power to rural areas, enabling greater participation in the digital economy.

Building trust is another critical component of overcoming barriers to data utilization. This involves not only protecting privacy and ensuring data security but also demonstrating the tangible benefits of data-driven approaches. Success stories from sectors like fintech, healthcare, and agriculture can help change perceptions and build momentum for broader adoption. Transparency is key; by sharing the results of data-driven initiatives and involving citizens in the process, Nigeria can foster trust and encourage greater engagement.

Ultimately, overcoming the barriers to data utilization in Nigeria requires a coordinated and collaborative effort from all stakeholders. The government, private sector, civil society, and international partners must work together to create an enabling environment for data-driven innovation. By addressing infrastructural deficits, building capacity, and promoting a culture of trust and transparency, Nigeria can overcome the obstacles that currently stand in its way and pave the path toward a brighter, data-driven future. In the next chapter, we will explore the role of education in building a data-savvy workforce and fostering a culture of innovation in Nigeria.

6.1 Strengthening Public-Private Partnerships for Data Development

One of the most effective ways to overcome the barriers to data utilization in Nigeria is through robust public-private partnerships (PPPs). Collaboration between government agencies, private organizations, and international stakeholders can accelerate the development of a cohesive data ecosystem by pooling resources, expertise, and technology. These partnerships are especially critical in addressing the infrastructural deficits that hinder data collection, analysis, and dissemination, which remain a significant challenge to the country's digital transformation.

Telecom companies, for instance, can partner with the government to expand broadband networks to underserved and rural areas. Leveraging public funding and private expertise, such collaborations can bring high-speed internet to regions where connectivity is sparse or non-existent. These efforts could include innovative approaches like deploying satellite internet, community-based wireless networks, or mobile hotspots powered by renewable energy. The impact of these initiatives extends far beyond improved connectivity, it also paves the way for increased participation in the digital economy, better access to online education, and the delivery of remote healthcare services.

Similarly, energy providers can collaborate on projects to enhance the reliability of the power supply, which is crucial for the operation of data centers and other digital infrastructure. By investing in renewable energy sources such as solar, wind, and hydroelectric power, these partnerships can create sustainable solutions that not only meet the energy demands of a growing data ecosystem but also contribute to environmental goals. For instance, a PPP initiative could establish solar-powered data hubs in rural areas, ensuring that even the most remote communities have access to critical digital services.

Private sector actors also have a significant role in building centralized data repositories. By sharing anonymized datasets that complement government-collected data, they can contribute to a more comprehensive understanding of Nigeria's economic and social dynamics. Financial institutions, for example, could provide insights into consumer spending patterns, while e-commerce platforms might share data on purchasing trends and preferences. Logistics companies could contribute information about supply chain efficiency, while mobile network operators could provide geolocation data to track migration trends or population density. These datasets, when combined with public sector information, would create a holistic view of Nigeria's landscape, enabling data-driven policies, targeted interventions, and innovative business solutions.

International development organizations and tech firms are valuable partners in advancing Nigeria's data ecosystem. By providing technical expertise, funding, and advanced tools, these entities can help Nigeria leapfrog traditional developmental hurdles and adopt innovative technologies. For instance, partnerships with global cloud service providers can enable the deployment of scalable, secure platforms for data storage and processing. Similarly, collaborations with AI and machine learning firms can introduce predictive analytics tools that help government agencies and businesses make more informed decisions. International partnerships could also support the training of Nigerian professionals, ensuring a steady pipeline of skilled data scientists, engineers, and technologists.

The success of PPPs in Nigeria ultimately depends on clear agreements that prioritize data sovereignty, ethical use, and equitable benefits for all stakeholders. Establishing frameworks that define the roles and responsibilities of each party ensures transparency and accountability. Policies that emphasize the localization of data storage, the protection of citizens' privacy, and the fair distribution of economic benefits can build trust and foster long-term collaboration.

These partnerships can also stimulate innovation by integrating global best practices into Nigeria's data development efforts. For instance, PPPs could fund pilot programs to test the feasibility of new technologies, such as blockchain for secure data management or IoT devices for monitoring infrastructure. By scaling successful pilots, Nigeria can accelerate its digital transformation and position itself as a leader in the region's data economy.

6.2 Encouraging Innovation Through Incentives and Competitions

Fostering a culture of data-driven innovation requires targeted incentives and initiatives that encourage individuals and organizations to embrace data as a transformative tool. One of the most effective strategies to achieve this goal is organizing competitions and hackathons that challenge participants to develop creative, data-driven solutions to real-world problems. These events not only inspire innovation but also provide a platform for discovering and nurturing talent, fostering collaboration, and driving the adoption of data-centric practices.

For example, a government-sponsored hackathon could focus on using data to address pressing issues in sectors such as healthcare, agriculture, education, and urban planning. Participants, including students, entrepreneurs, and tech professionals, could compete to design innovative solutions such as predictive analytics tools for disease outbreak management, mobile apps that connect farmers to markets, or data visualization platforms that help policymakers allocate resources effectively. Winning teams could receive funding, mentorship from industry experts, and opportunities to pilot their solutions with government agencies or private sector partners. Such initiatives could uncover groundbreaking ideas and provide a clear pathway for scaling them into impactful solutions.

Beyond competitions, financial incentives such as grants, tax breaks, and subsidies can encourage businesses to invest in data-driven technologies. For instance, small and medium-sized enterprises (SMEs) that adopt advanced analytics tools or develop data-focused projects could qualify for reduced tax rates or access to low-interest loans. These financial incentives lower the barriers to entry for smaller businesses, enabling them to compete with larger, more established firms. Additionally, dedicated funds for data-driven innovation could be established, targeting high-growth sectors like fintech, Agri-tech, and ed-tech.

Establishing innovation hubs and data centers in strategic locations across Nigeria can also serve as catalysts for data-driven growth. These hubs could provide entrepreneurs, researchers, and developers with access to state-of-the-art facilities, mentorship programs, and funding opportunities. Innovation hubs could include shared workspaces equipped with high-performance computing resources, training centers offering courses on data analytics and software development, and incubators that support early-stage startups. Partnerships with universities and research institutions can further enhance these hubs, ensuring access to the latest tools, knowledge, and talent pipelines.

Incentive-driven initiatives could also include public recognition programs that celebrate data-driven innovation. Awards for excellence in data utilization, ranging from startups to government projects, could highlight best practices and inspire others to follow suit. For example, an annual "Nigeria Data Innovation Awards" could showcase projects that demonstrate exceptional impact in areas such as public health, environmental conservation, and urban development.

To ensure widespread participation in these initiatives, outreach programs should be implemented to raise awareness about the opportunities available. Workshops, webinars, and social media campaigns can encourage diverse groups, including women, youth, and individuals from underserved communities to participate in competitions, training programs, and funding opportunities. This inclusivity ensures that data-driven innovation benefits all segments of society, fostering equitable growth and development.

Encouraging innovation through incentives and competitions not only accelerates the adoption of data-driven practices but also strengthens Nigeria's position as a leader in the digital economy. By creating an environment that rewards creativity and collaboration, the nation can unlock its full potential in leveraging data to drive economic growth, improve public services, and enhance quality of life. These initiatives, supported by partnerships, education, and robust infrastructure, will be instrumental in shaping Nigeria's data-driven future.

CHAPTER 7
THE ROLE OF EDUCATION IN BUILDING DATA LITERACY

Education is the bedrock of any nation's development, and in a rapidly evolving digital age, it is essential to equip citizens with the skills and knowledge needed to navigate a data-driven world. In Nigeria, the integration of data literacy into the educational system is not just an opportunity it is an urgent necessity. From primary schools to universities, and across vocational and professional training programs, education must be at the forefront of Nigeria's efforts to build a workforce capable of harnessing the power of data.

Data literacy goes beyond the ability to read and interpret numbers; it encompasses a broad set of skills, including data collection, analysis, visualization, and ethical decision-making. These competencies are vital for a wide range of careers, from data science and software engineering to public policy and business management. In a country like Nigeria, where unemployment remains high and many sectors are still adapting to digital transformation, fostering data literacy can open doors to new opportunities and drive economic diversification.

The foundation for data literacy must be laid early, starting in primary and secondary schools. Unfortunately, the current Nigerian education system faces significant challenges, including outdated curricula, inadequate infrastructure, and a shortage of qualified teachers. In many schools, particularly those in rural areas, access to computers and the internet is limited or nonexistent, making it difficult to introduce digital skills. To address these issues, Nigeria must prioritize investments in educational technology and teacher training. Programs that provide schools with affordable laptops, internet access, and interactive learning platforms can help bridge the digital divide and create an environment where data literacy can thrive.

Incorporating data science and computational thinking into school curricula is another critical step. Students should be introduced to basic concepts such as data collection, statistics, and coding from an early age, with more advanced topics like machine learning and artificial intelligence introduced in later years. These subjects should not be treated as standalone courses but integrated across disciplines, demonstrating how data is relevant to fields as diverse as mathematics, biology, geography, and economics. For example, a biology lesson on ecosystems could include exercises in data analysis, teaching students how to interpret graphs and draw conclusions from real-world data.

Beyond primary and secondary education, Nigeria's universities and vocational training institutions must play a central role in building a data-savvy workforce. Many Nigerian universities already offer programs in computer science, engineering, and related fields, but the focus on practical, hands-on data skills is often limited. To address this gap, universities must collaborate with industry partners to develop curricula that reflect the demands of the modern workforce. Internships, project-based learning, and partnerships with tech companies can provide students with real-world experience and prepare them for careers in data-driven industries.

Vocational training programs are particularly important for addressing the needs of individuals who are already in the workforce or who may not have access to traditional higher education. Short-term courses and certification programs in data analysis, coding, and digital marketing can provide valuable skills that enable workers to transition into higher-paying, tech-oriented roles. These programs should be accessible and affordable, with options for online learning to accommodate those in remote or underserved areas.

Another key component of fostering data literacy is raising awareness about the importance of data in everyday life. Public education campaigns, community workshops, and online resources can help demystify data and show how it can be used to solve practical problems. For example, a farmer might learn how to use weather data to plan their planting schedule, or a small business owner might discover how to use analytics tools to track sales trends.

By making data literacy relevant to people's daily lives, Nigeria can build a culture that values and embraces data-driven decision-making.

Teacher training is essential for the success of these initiatives. Teachers are the primary facilitators of learning, and their ability to effectively teach data-related subjects depends on their own understanding of the material. Professional development programs, both online and in-person, should be designed to equip teachers with the skills and confidence they need to integrate data literacy into their classrooms. Additionally, creating a network of educators who can share the best practices and resources will foster collaboration and innovation in teaching.

Government support and policy frameworks are critical for scaling these efforts. Ministries of Education at both federal and state levels must prioritize data literacy in their strategic plans, allocating funding and resources to support its implementation. Policies that incentivize schools and universities to adopt data-centric curricula, as well as partnerships with private sector organizations, can accelerate progress. Furthermore, national standards for data education can ensure consistency and quality across institutions.

The private sector also has a vital role to play in advancing data literacy in Nigeria. Tech companies, NGOs, and international development organizations can contribute by providing resources, expertise, and funding for educational programs. Initiatives such as hackathons, coding bootcamps, and mentorship programs can inspire young Nigerians to pursue careers in technology and data science. Companies can also offer scholarships, internships, and job placement opportunities, creating pathways for students to transition from education to employment.

Finally, fostering a culture of lifelong learning is essential in a world where technology and data are constantly evolving. Data literacy is not a static skill but a dynamic one that requires continuous updating and adaptation. Encouraging individuals to seek ongoing education through online courses, professional certifications, and industry conferences will ensure that Nigeria's workforce remains competitive and future ready.

The integration of data literacy into Nigeria's education system is a long-term investment with far-reaching benefits. By equipping citizens with the skills to harness the power of data, Nigeria can unlock new opportunities for economic growth, innovation, and social progress. As the nation builds a data-savvy workforce, it will be better positioned to address its challenges and capitalize on its potential in a rapidly changing world. In the next chapter, we will delve into the ethical considerations and privacy concerns that arise in a data-driven society, exploring how Nigeria can strike a balance between innovation and responsibility.

7.1 Integrating Data Literacy into Informal Education Channels

While formal education systems are critical to building data literacy in Nigeria, the importance of informal education channels cannot be overlooked. Many Nigerians, particularly in rural areas or from low-income backgrounds, may not have access to traditional schooling or advanced educational programs. Leveraging informal education can ensure that data literacy reaches underserved populations, fostering inclusivity and equity in the data revolution. Expanding the scope and impact of informal education in data literacy requires a multifaceted approach that prioritizes accessibility, relevance, and community engagement.

Community learning centers can serve as hubs for informal education, providing access to resources such as computers, internet connectivity, and data-focused workshops. These centers could host programs tailored to local needs, teaching participants how to use data in agriculture, trade, or small-scale manufacturing. For instance, farmers might learn to analyze weather data, identify optimal planting times, and predict market demand for their crops, enabling them to make informed decisions and maximize their yields. Similarly, artisans and small-scale manufacturers could use data insights to understand consumer preferences, optimize pricing strategies, and improve product designs. These centers could also serve as venues for hands-on training in digital tools such as Excel, basic coding, and data visualization software, equipping participants with practical skills.

Additionally, mobile learning platforms can play a transformative role in expanding access to data education. With mobile phone penetration increasing rapidly across Nigeria, interactive apps and SMS-based courses can deliver data literacy content to even the most remote areas. For example, farmers in rural areas could receive weather forecasts and crop price updates via text messages, helping them make data-informed decisions. Mobile apps with gamified learning modules could teach users how to analyze data, interpret graphs, and apply basic statistical tools in an engaging and accessible way. These platforms could also offer certification programs, allowing participants to showcase their new skills to potential employers or collaborators.

Partnerships with local influencers, community leaders, and religious organizations can further amplify the reach of informal education initiatives. These trusted figures can help raise awareness about the importance of data literacy and encourage participation in programs, building a culture of learning within their communities. For example, a religious leader could highlight the practical benefits of data skills in sermons, while community influencers could use social media to share success stories of individuals who have transformed their lives through data literacy. Collaboration with women's groups, youth associations, and agricultural cooperatives can further extend the reach of these programs, ensuring that they address the specific needs of different demographic groups.

To ensure the sustainability of informal education initiatives, partnerships with private sector organizations and NGOs are essential. Companies could sponsor mobile learning platforms, provide funding for community learning centers, or offer mentorship programs for participants. NGOs could contribute by designing curricula, training instructors, and conducting impact assessments to refine program delivery. Government support in the form of grants, subsidies, and policy frameworks can further strengthen these efforts, creating an enabling environment for informal data education.

7.2 Promoting Gender Inclusion in Data Literacy Programs

Achieving gender equity in data literacy is essential for maximizing Nigeria's potential in a data-driven world. Women, who make up nearly half of Nigeria's population, are often underrepresented in technology and data-related fields due to systemic barriers such as cultural norms, limited access to education, and financial constraints. Addressing these disparities is crucial for ensuring that women can contribute to and benefit from the opportunities created by data-driven innovation. Expanding efforts to promote gender inclusion in data literacy requires targeted strategies, community engagement, and a commitment to dismantling systemic barriers.

Targeted programs designed to empower women and girls with data skills can have a profound impact. Initiatives like coding bootcamps or scholarships for women in STEM (science, technology, engineering, and mathematics) can encourage greater participation in data-related fields. Bootcamps could include hands-on training in programming languages like Python or R, workshops on data analysis tools like Tableau, and sessions on the ethical implications of data usage. Scholarships could support women pursuing degrees in data science, computer engineering, or other tech-related disciplines, reducing the financial burden and encouraging enrollment in these fields. Additionally, mentorship programs where successful female professionals in technology and data science guide and inspire young women can foster confidence and provide role models for aspiring students.

In addition to technical training, it is important to address the cultural and societal factors that discourage women from pursuing careers in technology. Public awareness campaigns that challenge stereotypes and highlight the achievements of women in data-driven industries can shift perceptions and encourage more girls to pursue these fields. For example, a national campaign featuring stories of Nigerian women who have excelled in data science, artificial intelligence, and entrepreneurship could inspire others to follow suit. These campaigns could also include school outreach programs where female professionals visit classrooms to share their experiences and provide career guidance.

Creating safe and supportive learning environments, both in schools and in informal settings, is essential for ensuring that women and girls feel welcome and valued in their pursuit of data literacy. Schools can establish gender-focused support groups, provide access to female instructors, and adopt policies that discourage discrimination and harassment. In informal settings, women-only training sessions or community groups can offer a space where participants feel comfortable asking questions, sharing experiences, and supporting one another. These inclusive environments can boost confidence and encourage more women to engage with data-focused programs.

Private sector partnerships can play a significant role in advancing gender inclusion. Companies can implement policies that prioritize hiring and training women in data-focused roles, creating pathways for professional development. For example, tech firms could establish internship programs specifically for women, offering them exposure to real-world data projects and the opportunity to work alongside industry experts. Funding for women-specific programs, such as grants for female entrepreneurs using data to grow their businesses, can drive economic empowerment and innovation. For instance, a female-led aggrotech startup might use data to optimize supply chains, access markets, and improve agricultural productivity.

Governments and NGOs can further support gender inclusion by providing funding, advocacy, and policy frameworks that address systemic inequalities. This could include establishing quotas for female participation in government-funded data literacy programs, offering childcare support to enable women to attend training sessions, and advocating for gender-sensitive curricula in schools and training centers.

By promoting gender inclusion in data literacy programs, Nigeria can unlock the full potential of its population, driving more equitable and sustainable growth. Empowering women and girls with data skills is not only a matter of fairness but also a strategic imperative for national development. Research consistently shows that increasing gender diversity in technology and innovation leads to better problem-solving, greater creativity, and improved economic outcomes.

Education is the cornerstone of building a data-literate society, and Nigeria stands at a critical juncture in its efforts to integrate data literacy across formal, informal, and inclusive education channels. By investing in technology, updating curricula, and fostering partnerships between the public and private sectors, Nigeria can ensure that its citizens are equipped with the skills needed to thrive in a data-driven world. Targeted initiatives, such as community-based learning centers and programs focused on empowering women, will further enhance inclusivity and equity.

CHAPTER 8
DATA ETHICS AND PRIVACY IN NIGERIA

As Nigeria moves toward a data-driven society, the importance of ethics and privacy cannot be overstated. Data is a powerful tool that can transform governance, businesses, and communities, but its misuse can lead to significant harm. From identity theft and surveillance to algorithmic bias and discrimination, the risks associated with data collection and usage are real and far-reaching. For Nigeria, which is at the cusp of its digital transformation, establishing a robust framework for data ethics and privacy is not just a necessity, it is a moral imperative.

At the heart of any discussion about data ethics lies the issue of trust. For data-driven systems to work effectively, individuals must trust that their data will be collected, stored, and used responsibly. However, in Nigeria, public trust in institutions both public and private is often low, fueled by corruption scandals, data breaches, and lack of transparency. This trust deficit poses a significant challenge to building a data-driven ecosystem. Citizens are less likely to share personal information if they fear it will be mishandled or exploited.

One of the foundational principles of data ethics is informed consent. People have the right to know how their data is being collected, why it is being collected, and how it will be used. Unfortunately, many Nigerians are unaware of their rights when it comes to data privacy, and consent is often obtained in ways that are neither transparent nor meaningful. For example, users may be asked to accept complex and lengthy terms and conditions without fully understanding the implications. Addressing this issue requires a cultural shift that prioritizes transparency and clear communication. Companies and organizations must adopt practices that make it easy for individuals to understand and control how their data is used.

Another ethical concern is the risk of bias and discrimination in data-driven systems. Algorithms are often seen as objective tools, but they are only as unbiased as the data they are trained on. In Nigeria, where societal inequalities are deeply entrenched, there is a risk that data systems could perpetuate or even exacerbate existing disparities. For instance, an algorithm used to determine loan eligibility might inadvertently disadvantage certain groups if the underlying data reflects historical biases. To mitigate these risks, developers and policymakers must ensure that data is representative and that algorithms are tested rigorously for fairness.

Privacy is another critical issue. As more personal data is collected and stored, the risk of breaches and misuse increases. In recent years, incidents of cybercrime in Nigeria have highlighted vulnerabilities in existing systems, from hacked databases to leaked personal information. These breaches not only harm individuals but also undermine public confidence in data-driven initiatives. Strengthening data security is therefore essential. Organizations must adopt best practices for encryption, access control, and cybersecurity, while the government must enforce regulations that hold entities accountable for data breaches.

The Nigeria Data Protection Regulation (NDPR), introduced in 2019, is a step in the right direction. It provides guidelines for data collection, storage, and processing, and establishes penalties for non-compliance. However, enforcement remains a challenge, with many organizations unaware of or unwilling to comply with the regulation. To address this, the government must invest in public awareness campaigns and capacity-building programs that help organizations understand their responsibilities under the NDPR. Additionally, the regulation should be updated regularly to address emerging challenges, such as the use of artificial intelligence and cross-border data flows.

International collaboration is also crucial for addressing ethical and privacy concerns. Data does not respect national boundaries, and Nigeria must align its policies with global standards to facilitate trade, investment, and innovation. Frameworks such as the General Data Protection Regulation (GDPR) in the European Union can serve as a model for developing robust privacy protections that balance individual rights with the need for innovation. By participating in international dialogues on data ethics and privacy, Nigeria can ensure that its policies are both forward-looking and globally relevant.

Public education is a key component of building a culture of data ethics. Many Nigerians are unaware of the risks and rights associated with data usage, leaving them vulnerable to exploitation. Schools, universities, and community organizations must play a role in raising awareness about data privacy and ethical practices. Workshops, online courses, and public service announcements can help individuals understand how to protect their data and make informed decisions about sharing it.

The private sector also has a responsibility to uphold ethical standards in data usage. Companies must adopt a "privacy by design" approach, embedding privacy considerations into every stage of product development. For instance, social media platforms and mobile apps should provide users with clear and intuitive controls for managing their data. Businesses should also conduct regular audits to ensure compliance with privacy regulations and ethical guidelines.

Transparency is a critical element of ethical data practices. Organizations must be open about how they collect and use data, and they must be willing to hold themselves accountable for any breaches or missteps. Transparency not only builds trust but also fosters innovation by encouraging collaboration and feedback from stakeholders. For example, a government agency that publishes anonymized datasets on healthcare or education can invite researchers and entrepreneurs to develop new solutions, creating value for society while maintaining ethical standards.

Data ethics is not just about mitigating risks, it is also about maximizing benefits. By adopting ethical practices, Nigeria can build a data ecosystem that is inclusive, equitable, and sustainable. For example, ethical data sharing can enable collaboration across sectors, leading to innovations that improve healthcare, education, and economic development. Similarly, privacy-conscious data systems can empower individuals to take control of their personal information, fostering a sense of agency and trust.

As Nigeria embarks on its data journey, the ethical and privacy challenges it faces are significant, but they are not insurmountable. By prioritizing transparency, fairness, and accountability, the nation can build a data-driven society that respects individual rights while driving progress. In the next chapter, we will explore real-world success stories from Nigeria, showcasing how data has already begun to transform lives and industries, and highlighting the lessons that can guide future initiatives.

8.1 Building Institutional Capacity for Ethical Data Governance

The foundation of any robust data ethics and privacy framework lies in the strength of the institutions responsible for governance. In Nigeria, building institutional capacity is essential to ensure that data is collected, stored, and utilized in ways that respect individual rights and promote societal good. While regulations such as the Nigeria Data Protection Regulation (NDPR) provide a strong starting point, their effectiveness depends on the capacity of enforcement agencies and institutions to uphold these standards across all sectors and adapt to emerging challenges in the rapidly evolving digital landscape.

A critical first step is the establishment of a dedicated data ethics and privacy commission with the authority to oversee compliance, investigate breaches, and impose penalties. This commission should operate as an independent body with the resources and mandate to regulate data practices across government, private sector, and civil society. Staffed with experts in law, technology, ethics, and data science, the commission can take a multidisciplinary approach to governance. Its responsibilities could include providing technical guidance on compliance with data protection laws, auditing organizations' data practices, and publishing annual reports on the state of data ethics and privacy in Nigeria. Additionally, this body can play a proactive role in identifying emerging trends and risks, ensuring that the regulatory framework evolves in step with technological advancements.

Capacity-building initiatives for public sector institutions are equally important. Government agencies that collect and manage data must adopt standardized protocols for ethical data handling. Training programs tailored for civil servants, policymakers, and IT administrators can raise awareness of privacy considerations and equip them with the skills to implement secure and transparent data practices. For example, workshops could cover topics such as encryption methods, access control mechanisms, and privacy impact assessments. Partnering with academic institutions can further enhance capacity by providing access to innovative research and fostering a culture of continuous improvement. Universities could also collaborate with government agencies to develop certification programs in data governance and privacy, creating a skilled workforce dedicated to ethical data management.

Investment in technology infrastructure is another critical element. Modern tools for data encryption, secure storage, and access control must be deployed to protect sensitive information from breaches. Institutions must also establish clear frameworks for data sharing, outlining who can access what data, under what conditions, and for what purposes. These frameworks should include provisions for anonymization and pseudonymization to protect individual identities in shared datasets. Moreover, mechanisms for auditing and accountability must be embedded into data governance structures to ensure that ethical standards are consistently upheld. Regular third-party audits can provide transparency and build public trust in institutional data practices.

Public awareness campaigns are also essential for building institutional capacity. Educating citizens about their rights under data protection laws and encouraging them to report breaches or unethical practices can create a bottom-up pressure that complements institutional enforcement. Transparency initiatives, such as open data portals that allow the public to monitor government data usage, can further enhance accountability and build trust in data-driven initiatives.

8.2 Addressing Ethical Challenges in Emerging Technologies

Emerging technologies such as artificial intelligence (AI), machine learning, and biometric systems present new ethical challenges that require proactive measures to ensure their responsible development and deployment. While these technologies offer transformative potential for innovation and efficiency, they also raise complex concerns about bias, surveillance, and misuse. Building a framework for ethical governance of emerging technologies is critical for Nigeria to harness their benefits while safeguarding individual rights and social equity.

One of the most pressing issues is algorithmic bias. AI systems often reflect the biases present in their training data, which can lead to discriminatory outcomes. For example, an AI-based recruitment tool might disadvantage certain demographics if historical hiring data contains patterns of exclusion. Similarly, a credit scoring algorithm could inadvertently penalize applicants from underrepresented regions due to a lack of comprehensive data. In Nigeria, where social and economic inequalities are pervasive, unchecked algorithmic bias could exacerbate existing disparities. To address this, developers and organizations must prioritize fairness and inclusivity in algorithm design. This includes using diverse and representative datasets, conducting regular bias audits, and involving stakeholders from affected communities in the development process. Regulatory guidelines could mandate transparency in AI decision-making processes, requiring organizations to provide explanations for automated decisions that impact individuals.

Biometric systems, widely used for voter registration, national identification, and security applications, also require careful ethical consideration. While they offer significant advantages in preventing fraud and ensuring security, they can infringe on privacy if misused. For instance, biometric data collected for one purpose, such as national identification, should not be repurposed without explicit and informed consent. Clear regulations must define the acceptable use of biometric data, and robust security measures must be implemented to protect it from breaches. Institutions handling biometric data should adopt the highest standards of encryption and access control, and individuals should have the right to review and revoke consent for the use of their data.

Surveillance technologies present another area of concern. While tools like CCTV networks, facial recognition software, and social media monitoring can enhance public safety, excessive surveillance can infringe on civil liberties and foster distrust. Striking a balance between security and privacy requires transparent policies that define the scope and limits of surveillance. For example, laws should specify the duration for which surveillance data can be retained, who has access to it, and the conditions under which it can be shared or analyzed. Public oversight mechanisms, such as independent review boards, can ensure that surveillance practices remain accountable and aligned with ethical standards.

8.3 Fostering a Global Perspective on Data Ethics

As Nigeria navigates the complexities of data ethics and privacy, it must also consider its position in the global digital ecosystem. Data flows freely across borders and aligning with international standards is essential for fostering trust, facilitating trade, and attracting investment. Engaging in international dialogues and adopting globally recognized frameworks can help Nigeria address domestic challenges while enhancing its standing in the global data economy.

Collaborating with organizations such as the African Union and adopting frameworks like the EU's General Data Protection Regulation (GDPR) can provide valuable insights and establish Nigeria as a responsible player in the global data economy. For example, harmonizing Nigerian data protection laws with the GDPR could simplify compliance for multinational companies operating in Nigeria, encouraging foreign investment. Participation in initiatives such as the African Continental Free Trade Area (AfCFTA) could also promote equitable data sharing across the continent, enabling regional collaboration on data-driven projects in areas like healthcare, agriculture, and infrastructure development.

Participation in international forums on data ethics can also help Nigeria address challenges unique to developing economies. For example, discussions on equitable data sharing can ensure that Nigerian data is not exploited by more developed nations without delivering reciprocal benefits. By advocating for data-sharing agreements that prioritize local development, Nigeria can ensure that its resources are used to create value domestically. Furthermore, global partnerships can provide access to expertise and resources for addressing complex issues such as cross-border data transfers, AI ethics, and cybersecurity.

By adopting a global perspective, Nigeria can protect its citizens' rights while positioning itself as a leader in ethical data practices. This approach will enhance the nation's reputation, attract investment, and foster innovation. A robust, globally aligned data ethics framework can ensure that Nigeria remains competitive in the digital age while upholding its commitment to social responsibility and equity.

In conclusion, building institutional capacity, addressing ethical challenges in emerging technologies, and fostering a global perspective are essential for creating a sustainable and ethical data ecosystem in Nigeria. These efforts will ensure that the nation harnesses the full potential of data while safeguarding the rights and interests of its citizens.

CHAPTER 9
CASE STUDIES SUCCESS STORIES FROM NIGERIA

The transformative potential of data is no longer theoretical; it is already being realized in various sectors across Nigeria. From agriculture and healthcare to finance and education, data-driven initiatives are demonstrating how information, when effectively harnessed, can address critical challenges and create new opportunities. This chapter explores several success stories that highlight the power of data in action, offering valuable lessons for future endeavors.

One of the most celebrated examples of data-driven innovation in Nigeria is the rise of fintech. Companies like Flutter wave, Paystack, and Paga have revolutionized the way Nigerians access and interact with financial services. By leveraging data, these startups have not only improved the efficiency of transactions but also brought financial inclusion to millions of previously unbanked individuals. For instance, Flutter wave uses payment data to provide insights to merchants about consumer behavior, enabling them to optimize their operations. Similarly, Paystack employs machine learning algorithms to detect and prevent fraudulent transactions, safeguarding the financial ecosystem. These companies demonstrate how data can be a catalyst for economic growth, driving innovation and fostering trust in a sector that is critical to the nation's development.

In the agricultural sector, data helps farmers overcome longstanding challenges related to productivity and market access. Hello Tractor, often referred to as the "Uber for Tractors," connects smallholder farmers with tractor owners through a data-driven platform. By using GPS and predictive analytics, Hello Tractor ensures that tractors are deployed efficiently, reducing downtime and increasing farm yields. Farmers can also access weather data and market price trends through the platform, enabling them to make informed decisions about planting and selling their crops. This approach not only boosts agricultural productivity but also improves livelihoods, demonstrating how data can drive social and economic transformation in rural communities.

Healthcare is another sector where data has made a significant impact. During the COVID-19 pandemic, data played a crucial role in Nigeria's response efforts. The Nigeria Centre for Disease Control (NCDC) used data to track the spread of the virus, allocate resources, and inform public health policies. Dashboards displaying real-time data on infection rates and vaccination coverage helped policymakers make evidence-based decisions. Beyond the pandemic, organizations like LifeBank are leveraging data to address critical healthcare challenges. LifeBank uses GPS and real-time tracking to ensure the efficient delivery of blood, oxygen, and medical supplies to hospitals, saving countless lives in the process. These initiatives underscore the importance of data in building a resilient healthcare system capable of responding to both emergencies and everyday needs.

In the education sector, data-driven platforms are improving access to quality learning resources. Ed-tech companies like uLesson and Tuteria are using data to personalize learning experiences for students, adapting content to their individual strengths and weaknesses. For example, uLesson analyzes user engagement data to refine its digital lessons, ensuring that students stay motivated and achieve better outcomes. Tuteria connects students with tutors based on their specific needs and preferences, creating a tailored learning experience that maximizes impact. These platforms are breaking down barriers to education, particularly in underserved areas, and demonstrating how data can bridge gaps in access and quality.

The energy sector, too, has benefited from data-driven innovations. Nigeria's persistent electricity challenges have prompted creative solutions that leverage data to improve energy access and efficiency. Companies like Lumos and Rensource are using data to optimize the distribution and management of solar power systems, providing reliable energy to households and businesses. By analyzing consumption patterns, these companies can offer tailored energy solutions that meet the unique needs of their customers. In doing so, they are not only addressing energy poverty but also contributing to environmental sustainability.

Transportation and urban planning offer another compelling example of data-driven progress. In cities like Lagos, where traffic congestion is a daily challenge, platforms like Max.ng and Gokada are using data to optimize ride-hailing and delivery services. By analyzing traffic patterns and rider preferences, these companies ensure faster, more efficient transportation options. Additionally, data from ride-hailing platforms is being used by urban planners to identify bottlenecks and design more effective transportation systems. These innovations highlight the potential of data to improve quality of life in densely populated urban areas.

Despite these successes, the road to achieving meaningful data-driven transformation has not been without challenges. Many of these initiatives faced initial skepticism, infrastructural limitations, and regulatory hurdles. However, their ability to overcome these obstacles provides valuable insights for future projects. One key takeaway is the importance of collaboration. Whether it is partnerships between startups and government agencies or collaborations with international organizations, these initiatives have demonstrated that collective efforts are essential for scaling data-driven solutions.

Another critical lesson is the value of inclusivity. Many of these success stories have focused on underserved populations, proving that data can be a tool for social equity. By designing solutions that address the specific needs of marginalized groups, these initiatives have not only achieved commercial success but also created a broader societal impact. This inclusive approach should serve as a guiding principle for future data-driven projects in Nigeria.

Finally, these success stories highlight the importance of adaptability and resilience. The dynamic nature of data and technology means that challenges and opportunities are constantly evolving. Organizations that can adapt to changing circumstances, learn from their mistakes, and embrace innovation are better positioned to succeed overall.

As Nigeria continues its journey toward becoming a data-driven nation, these examples provide a roadmap for what is possible. They demonstrate that data is not an abstract concept but a tangible resource that can transform lives and industries. By building on these successes and scaling their impact, Nigeria can unlock new opportunities for growth, innovation, and progress. In the next chapter, we will synthesize the insights and strategies presented throughout this book, outlining a comprehensive blueprint for realizing Nigeria's data-driven future.

9.1 Leveraging Data for Environmental Sustainability

Another area where data-driven initiatives are making an impact in Nigeria is environmental sustainability. As the country grapples with deforestation, pollution, and climate change, data is emerging as a powerful tool for monitoring environmental challenges and implementing solutions. Expanding these initiatives and integrating advanced technologies into environmental policies can significantly enhance Nigeria's ability to address its ecological challenges while fostering economic growth and resilience.

Organizations such as **GreenHubAfrica** are at the forefront of leveraging geospatial data and satellite imagery to monitor environmental degradation. These tools provide real-time insights into deforestation and land degradation, enabling policymakers and stakeholders to identify areas most at risk. For example, satellite imagery can reveal illegal logging activities, monitor desertification in the northern regions, and assess the health of wetlands that are vital for biodiversity. By sharing these insights with government agencies, NGOs, and local communities, these initiatives pave the way for targeted interventions, such as reforestation projects, soil restoration programs, and the enforcement of environmental regulations. Scaling these efforts could involve partnerships with global organizations specializing in remote sensing and GIS technologies, further enhancing Nigeria's capacity to protect its natural resources.

The renewable energy sector is another domain where data is driving sustainability. Startups such as **Rubitec Solar** are using predictive analytics to design and optimize off-grid solar energy systems for rural and peri-urban communities. By analyzing a combination of weather patterns, population density, and energy consumption data, these companies deliver solutions that maximize energy efficiency while minimizing costs. Predictive models can also forecast energy demands, ensuring that renewable energy systems are scaled appropriately to meet future needs. These efforts reduce reliance on fossil fuels, cut greenhouse gas emissions, and contribute to Nigeria's commitments under the Paris Climate Agreement. To amplify the impact, data from renewable energy projects can be shared with national energy planners, enabling a more integrated and sustainable approach to addressing Nigeria's energy challenges.

Waste management is another critical area benefiting from data-driven approaches. Companies such as **Wecyclers** are revolutionizing recycling programs in urban areas by employing data to improve efficiency and participation. By tracking the volume, types, and locations of waste collected, these companies can identify trends and optimize collection routes to minimize operational costs and environmental impact. For example, data analytics can determine peak times for waste generation in specific neighborhoods, allowing for more effective scheduling of waste pickups. Additionally, mobile apps can be developed to encourage community engagement by allowing residents to track their recycling contributions and earn rewards. By integrating IoT-enabled sensors into waste bins, local governments can enhance data collection, creating a robust system for managing urban waste. These initiatives not only reduce pollution but also create economic opportunities by turning waste into resources through recycling and upcycling.

The application of data in combating pollution is another area with significant potential. Sensors installed in urban centers can monitor air and water quality in real time, providing critical data on pollutants and their sources. For instance, data from air quality sensors in Lagos could inform policies to regulate emissions from industrial zones and vehicles. Similarly, water quality monitoring in the Niger Delta can help address pollution from oil spills and industrial discharge, safeguarding public health and preserving aquatic ecosystems. Data-driven approaches can also support community-led environmental advocacy, enabling local groups to demand action and hold polluters accountable.

By expanding the use of data-driven environmental policies, Nigeria can unlock innovative solutions to its ecological challenges. Partnerships with international organizations and private sector stakeholders can provide funding, expertise, and access to advanced technologies. Public awareness campaigns highlighting the role of data in sustainability can further galvanize support from citizens and businesses, fostering a culture of environmental stewardship.

9.2 Data-Driven Governance: The Example of Budget Transparency

In governance, data is playing an increasingly important role in promoting transparency, accountability, and public participation. Platforms such as **BudgIT** have transformed how Nigerians engage with public finances, demonstrating the potential of data-driven governance to enhance democratic institutions and improve resource allocation. Expanding on these successes, Nigeria can further leverage data to strengthen its governance systems and empower citizens.

BudgIT employs data visualization tools to simplify complex budget information, making it accessible to citizens regardless of their education or background. This accessibility allows individuals to understand how public funds are allocated and spent, bridging the gap between the government and its constituents. For example, interactive dashboards can highlight discrepancies in government spending, such as funds allocated to a road construction project that remains incomplete. By presenting this information in an easy-to-digest format, BudgIT empowers citizens to question public officials, demand accountability, and advocate for more equitable distribution of resources.

The Open Budget platform extends BudgIT's impact by enabling real-time monitoring of government projects. Citizens can report on the status of infrastructure projects in their communities, such as roads, schools, or healthcare facilities, providing feedback directly to authorities. For instance, if a school renovation project has been delayed despite funds being allocated, residents can document the delay and escalate the issue. This crowdsourced approach to governance ensures that public officials remain accountable and that resources are used efficiently. Furthermore, the data collected through citizen feedback can be aggregated and analyzed to identify systemic bottlenecks in project delivery, guiding policymakers in implementing reforms.

The success of platforms like BudgIT underscores the potential of data to build trust between citizens and the state. By fostering transparency, these initiatives reduce opportunities for corruption and mismanagement, which have long plagued Nigeria's public sector. They also encourage active citizenship, where individuals feel empowered to participate in governance processes. This shift from passive observation to active engagement is critical for strengthening democratic institutions and ensuring that governance reflects the needs and priorities of the people.

Expanding data-driven governance requires scaling initiatives like BudgIT to cover additional areas of public administration, such as healthcare spending, education outcomes, and environmental programs. For example, a similar platform could be developed to track the disbursement of funds for healthcare facilities, allowing citizens to monitor improvements in service delivery. Additionally, integrating these platforms with government databases can streamline data collection and ensure that information is up-to-date and comprehensive.

Capacity-building for government officials is also essential for the success of data-driven governance. Training programs can equip public servants with the skills needed to manage and interpret data, enabling them to make evidence-based decisions. For example, local government officials could learn to use data analytics to identify underserved areas and allocate resources more effectively. Moreover, fostering partnerships between government agencies, tech startups, and international organizations can provide access to advanced tools and expertise, further enhancing the impact of data-driven governance.

Ultimately, data-driven governance represents a transformative opportunity for Nigeria to enhance transparency, accountability, and public trust. By expanding platforms like BudgIT, investing in capacity-building, and fostering public participation, the nation can build a governance system that is responsive, inclusive, and aligned with the aspirations of its citizens. These efforts not only strengthen Nigeria's democracy but also create a foundation for sustainable development and social progress.

CHAPTER 10
THE NIGERIAN DATA BLUEPRINT STEPS FORWARD

As we arrive at the conclusion of this book, it is clear that data holds the key to Nigeria's future. The transformative stories we have explored, the challenges we have examined, and the strategies we have discussed all point to one undeniable truth: data is a strategic asset that can propel Nigeria into a new era of development, innovation, and global competitiveness. However, unlocking this potential requires deliberate action, coordination, and vision. This final chapter outlines a comprehensive blueprint for building a sustainable and inclusive data-driven future for Nigeria.

The first pillar of this blueprint is infrastructure development. Reliable infrastructure forms the backbone of any data ecosystem, and Nigeria must prioritize investments in this area. This includes expanding internet connectivity, particularly in underserved rural areas, to bridge the digital divide. Initiatives like community broadband networks and public-private partnerships can accelerate progress, ensuring that no region is left behind. Additionally, data centers and cloud computing infrastructure must be scaled to support the storage and processing of vast amounts of information. Reliable electricity is another critical component, and investments in renewable energy can provide sustainable solutions to power the nation's digital transformation.

The second pillar is education and capacity-building. Data literacy must become a national priority, integrated into every level of education. From primary schools to universities, curricula should emphasize computational thinking, data analysis, and digital skills. Vocational training programs should target individuals already in the workforce, equipping them with the tools they need to adapt to a data-driven economy. Beyond formal education, public awareness campaigns can demystify data for citizens, showing how it can improve their daily lives and foster a culture of informed decision-making.

The third pillar is policy and regulation. Clear and enforceable policies are essential for ensuring that data is used responsibly and ethically. The Nigeria Data Protection Regulation (NDPR) provides a foundation, but it must be strengthened and expanded to address emerging challenges such as artificial intelligence, cross-border data flows, and algorithmic bias. Transparency and accountability must be embedded in all data governance frameworks, fostering public trust and encouraging greater participation in data-driven initiatives.

The fourth pillar is collaboration and partnerships. No single entity can build a data-driven Nigeria alone. Collaboration between government agencies, private sector organizations, academia, and civil society is essential. The government must take the lead in creating an enabling environment, but the private sector can drive innovation and scale solutions. Partnerships with international organizations and development agencies can provide additional resources, expertise, and funding. By working together, stakeholders can create a cohesive data ecosystem that benefits all Nigerians.

The fifth pillar is inclusive growth and equity. Data-driven initiatives must prioritize inclusivity, ensuring that marginalized groups are not left behind. Women, rural communities, and individuals with limited digital access must be actively included in Nigeria's data journey. For example, targeted programs can provide training and resources for women entrepreneurs, empowering them to use data to grow their businesses. Similarly, community-based data projects can address the specific needs of rural areas, improving access to healthcare, education, and economic opportunities.

The sixth pillar is innovation and entrepreneurship. Data is a catalyst for creativity, and Nigeria's vibrant tech ecosystem is well-positioned to drive innovation. Startups and SMEs should be supported through funding, mentorship, and access to open data platforms. Hackathons, innovation hubs, and accelerator programs can inspire new ideas and foster collaboration. By creating an environment that nurtures innovation, Nigeria can build a thriving ecosystem of data-driven businesses that contribute to economic diversification and job creation.

The seventh pillar is monitoring and evaluation. Building a data-driven Nigeria is a long-term process, and progress must be tracked consistently to ensure accountability and success. Key performance indicators (KPIs) should be established for each sector, measuring outcomes such as increased internet penetration, improved literacy rates, and enhanced public service delivery. Regular audits and reviews can identify gaps and guide course corrections, ensuring that Nigeria stays on track to achieve its data-driven goals.

The final pillar is cultural transformation. Beyond infrastructure and policies, building a data-driven society requires a shift in mindset. Citizens, businesses, and government officials must recognize the value of data and embrace its use as a tool for progress. This cultural shift will take time, but it is essential for ensuring the sustainability of Nigeria's data journey. Celebrating success stories, fostering public dialogue, and highlighting the tangible benefits of data-driven initiatives can help build momentum and inspire collective action.

The Nigerian Data Blueprint is ambitious, but it is also achievable. By focusing on these eight pillars, Nigeria can build a data ecosystem that drives innovation, fosters inclusivity, and improves quality of life for all citizens. The journey will not be without challenges, but the rewards are well worth the effort. A data-driven Nigeria is not just a possibility; it is an inevitability if the nation commits to the steps outlined in this blueprint.

10.1 Prioritizing Sustainability in Nigeria's Data Blueprint

While the eight pillars outlined in the Nigerian Data Blueprint form a comprehensive strategy, a critical underlying theme must be **sustainability**. Building a data-driven society is not a short-term endeavor; it requires long-term planning and resilience to ensure that the progress made today benefits future generations. Sustainability in this context extends beyond environmental considerations to encompass economic and social dimensions, creating a holistic framework that drives enduring development.

Environmental Sustainability

Investments in infrastructure, such as data centers and energy grids, must incorporate environmentally sustainable practices. Data centers, which are essential for processing and storing vast amounts of information, are significant consumers of energy. Without careful planning, their energy demands could exacerbate Nigeria's existing challenges with electricity access and environmental degradation. Nigeria has an opportunity to lead by example by prioritizing renewable energy sources, such as solar, wind, and hydroelectric power, to meet the energy needs of these facilities. By integrating renewable solutions, Nigeria can establish green data centers that contribute to global climate goals while ensuring reliable operations.

Public-private partnerships can play a pivotal role in funding and operationalizing sustainable data centers. For example, partnerships between energy providers, technology companies, and government agencies could lead to the development of hybrid energy systems that combine solar power with advanced battery storage technologies. These partnerships can also attract foreign investment by demonstrating Nigeria's commitment to green technology, positioning the nation as a pioneer in environmentally conscious data infrastructure.

Beyond infrastructure, data itself can be a powerful tool for promoting environmental sustainability. Geospatial analytics, combined with machine learning, can monitor and predict deforestation patterns, urban sprawl, and air and water quality. For instance, policymakers could use satellite imagery to identify illegal logging activities in the Niger Delta or assess the impact of urbanization on agricultural lands. By incorporating these insights into policymaking, Nigeria can implement targeted measures to protect its natural resources, such as expanding protected areas, enforcing anti-pollution regulations, and incentivizing sustainable agricultural practices.

Community-led environmental initiatives powered by data can further enhance sustainability efforts. For example, local groups could use mobile apps to report environmental hazards, such as illegal dumping or oil spills, enabling authorities to respond swiftly. Additionally, educational campaigns leveraging data visualization tools could raise awareness about the long-term impacts of climate change and pollution, fostering a culture of environmental stewardship.

Economic Sustainability

Economic sustainability is equally critical to the success of Nigeria's data-driven future. A robust data economy requires continuous investment and innovation to thrive and ensuring that data-driven initiatives generate tangible economic value is essential for long-term viability. By fostering entrepreneurship and creating incentives for local tech companies, Nigeria can cultivate a self-sustaining ecosystem that reduces reliance on foreign funding and expertise.

Incentives such as tax breaks, grants, and access to affordable credit can encourage startups to develop innovative data-driven solutions in key sectors, including agriculture, healthcare, and education. For instance, aggrotech companies could use data to improve supply chain efficiency, connecting farmers directly with buyers to maximize profits and minimize waste. Similarly, edtech platforms could use analytics to personalize learning experiences, improving educational outcomes, and creating new revenue streams.

Data-driven fintech solutions also have immense potential to support economic sustainability. Services such as microloans, digital wallets, and blockchain-based financial platforms empower small businesses and individuals, particularly those in underserved communities. For example, a digital credit platform could analyze alternative data sources, such as mobile payment histories and social media activity, to extend loans to individuals without traditional credit histories. By increasing financial inclusion, these initiatives drive economic growth, reduce poverty, and create a virtuous cycle where economic empowerment supports the expansion of the data ecosystem.

Additionally, the development of a skilled workforce is critical for sustaining Nigeria's data economy. Investments in data literacy programs, vocational training, and partnerships with academic institutions can equip Nigerians with the skills needed to thrive in a data-driven job market. Creating opportunities for continuous learning ensures that the workforce remains adaptable to technological advancements, further bolstering economic resilience.

Social Sustainability

The Nigerian Data Blueprint must also prioritize social sustainability by addressing systemic inequalities and ensuring that data benefits all segments of society. Without deliberate efforts to bridge digital divides, there is a risk that marginalized groups including women, rural communities, and individuals with disabilities will be left behind in the data revolution. Programs designed to target these populations are essential for fostering inclusivity and equity.

Education and training initiatives must be tailored to reach all Nigerians, not just those in urban or affluent areas. For example, community learning centers equipped with computers and internet access could provide rural populations with opportunities to learn data skills. Mobile learning platforms, which deliver content via smartphones, can further expand access to education, ensuring that even the most remote communities can participate in the digital economy.

Transparency and accountability are foundational to social sustainability. Data-driven governance initiatives must actively involve citizens in decision-making processes, ensuring that the benefits of data-driven policies are distributed fairly and visibly. Platforms that allow citizens to monitor government projects, report issues, and provide feedback can strengthen trust in public institutions. For example, a community monitoring system could enable residents to track the progress of local infrastructure projects, such as the construction of schools or healthcare centers, fostering a sense of shared responsibility and civic engagement.

Programs that promote gender inclusion are particularly important for achieving social sustainability. Initiatives that support women in tech, provide scholarships for data-related fields, and create mentorship networks can help bridge gender gaps in the data economy. Empowering women and girls with data skills not only contributes to economic growth but also strengthens social cohesion by addressing historical inequalities.

10.2 A Vision for Nigeria's Data-Driven Future

The Nigerian Data Blueprint provides a clear and actionable path forward, but its ultimate success depends on the collective will of the nation. Achieving a data-driven Nigeria will require visionary leadership, cross-sector collaboration, and a commitment to continuous improvement. By prioritizing sustainability across environmental, economic, and social dimensions, Nigeria can ensure that its data initiatives deliver lasting benefits for all citizens.

Imagine a Nigeria where farmers use real-time data to optimize their harvests, urban planners design smart cities powered by predictive analytics, and students in remote villages access world-class education through digital platforms. Picture a healthcare system capable of tracking and addressing diseases before they become epidemics, and a financial sector that empowers every Nigerian to participate in the economy, regardless of location or income.

This vision is not a distant dream, it is an attainable reality. With deliberate action and unwavering commitment, Nigeria can transform its data potential into tangible progress, emerging as a leader in the global digital economy. The time to act is now. Through the collective efforts of government, industry, and citizens, Nigeria can turn this blueprint into a legacy of innovation, equity, and resilience.

The journey ahead may be challenging, but the destination, a Nigeria empowered by data, united by purpose, and ready to embrace the opportunities of a data-driven world is well worth the effort.

REVIEWS

"An indispensable guide for anyone invested in Nigeria's future. Shefiu Yusuf has masterfully outlined how data can transform industries, governance, and society at large. This book is a must-read for policymakers, entrepreneurs, and educators alike.

— Prof. Adenike Oke, Chair of Data and Innovation, University of Lagos

"Shefiu Yusuf's vision for a data-driven Nigeria is both inspiring and practical. This book doesn't just highlight the challenges we face; it provides actionable solutions that can drive real progress."

— Kola Adebayo, CEO, TechSolve Africa

"A significant change for the African continent. The Nigerian Data Blueprint offers a comprehensive roadmap for how countries can harness the power of data to achieve sustainable growth and inclusivity."

— Dr. Grace Eze, Economist and Development Specialist

"This book demonstrates the transformative potential of data in every sector. Shefiu Yusuf has created a blueprint that should be on the desk of every policymaker and business leader in Nigeria."

— Amaka Onwugbufor, Founder, Data for Good Initiative

"Shefiu Yusuf's work is a wake-up call for those who underestimate the value of data. This book is a treasure trove of insights, strategies, and real-world examples."

— Daniel Olumide, Author of Building Africa's Digital Future

ABOUT THE AUTHOR

S hefiu Yusuf is a passionate advocate for leveraging data to drive meaningful change in society. With a background in data science and a deep commitment to fostering innovation, he has dedicated his career to exploring the intersections of technology, governance, and economic development. His work spans over a decade, during which he has collaborated with governments, private organizations, and educational institutions to build data-driven solutions tailored to the unique challenges of Nigeria and the African continent.

His journey into the world of data began early in his academic career, where he studied computer science and specialized in data analytics. Over time, he developed a keen interest in how data could be used not just as a technical resource but as a strategic tool for empowering communities, improving governance, and driving economic progress. This vision has guided his work, from consulting on large-scale data projects to mentoring young professionals seeking to make their mark in the field.

As a thought leader, he has authored numerous articles and delivered keynote speeches on the transformative power of data. He is a strong proponent of open data initiatives, ethical data practices, and the integration of data literacy into educational systems. His work has earned recognition both locally and internationally, cementing his reputation as one of Nigeria's leading voices in the data revolution.

When he is not working on data-related projects, he enjoys mentoring the next generation of tech innovators, engaging with communities to promote digital inclusion, and exploring the ways in which technology can create a more equitable society. **The Nigerian Data Blueprint** is a culmination of his insights, experiences, and aspirations for a future where data serves as a force for good.